The Gift of Guilt;

10 Steps to Freedom from Guilt, Forever

Expanded Edition

BY

SHANNON MILLER, BCBC

The Gift of Guilt; 10 Steps To Freedom From Guilt, Forever

Expanded Edition

Published by "LuLu (www.lulu.com), the world's fastest-growing provider of print-on-demand books."

ISBN 978-1-84728-861-5

"Scripture quotations taken from the New American Standard Bible ®, Copyright © 1960, 1962, 1963, 1968, 1971, 1973, 1975, 1977, 1995 by The Lockman Foundation. Used by permission. (www.Lockman.org)

Scripture quotations taken from the Holy Bible, New International Version ®. Copyright © 1973, 1978, 1984 International Bible Society. Used by permission of Zondervan. All rights reserved. Scripture from the King James Version. Copyright © 1984, 1977 Thomas Nelson, Inc.

Dedication

This book is dedicated to the hurting people out there who are struggling to get through life in the best way they know how. I pray this helps: it was written for you.

My Thanks

There are so many people who have helped me along the way, I could never name them all. Forgive me if you are not specifically mentioned, you know who you are, I love you.

I never would have had the courage to complete this book without the hard work and encouragement of Dr. Robert Kilmer, my creative writing professor at Northern Virginia Community College. Robert convinced me that my brain could still function despite the many years of lying dormant. Robert and I went over the first draft of this book, word by word, until we were both sick of it! Thank you my dear friend!

My husband Jonathan and children Kimberly and Joshua have endured countless hours of neglect as I have listened to people tell me their stories and tried to help them make some sense of it all. I can never fully express how much your love and support has meant over these many years. You are all simply the best!

I also want to thank my mother, Allyn D. Smith. Mom died of breast cancer when I was just nineteen-years-old. She was a professional writer, yet she never finished the book that was in her head. Mom's disappointment in herself taught me to be less fearful of my own need to write.

Finally, I want to thank all the women who have shared their problems with me for almost thirty years. It has always been an honor to be trusted with your secrets.

Part I: Guilt; Gift or Curse?

Chapter One

It All Seems Like One Big Curse to Me!

"Come to me, all ye who are weary and heavy-laden, and I will give you rest. Take My yoke upon you and learn from Me, for I am gentle and humble in heart, and you will find rest for your souls." (NASB)

I had been a Christian for just a few months when the pastor of my church called and asked me to talk with a woman I had never met. Julie came to church every Sunday, sat on the back pew with her young daughter, and raced out to her car as soon as the service was ended. Few people even knew her name. She had refused the minister's offer of a pastoral visit, so he was hoping that she might open up to a woman.

I managed to get an invitation to Julie's house on the pretext of our daughters having a play date. Julie was too thin, her dark eyes darted from spot to spot, never holding eye contact with me for more than a brief moment. I had no idea where to start, so I did what came naturally to me; I began talking.

I talked mostly about myself and, in particular, my trashy life before becoming a Christian. I also shared information about the sins I had struggled with *after* giving my life over to Jesus. I was thirty-years-old before I was introduced to Jesus as Lord and Savior. No one handed me a pamphlet titled *How to Act Like a Christian Woman* at my conversion. Old habits die hard and I needed the Holy Spirit to gently lead me away from my behaviors, not beat me up with the whole mess all at once! Julie was so relieved to hear me admit that I had struggled with sexual sin even after becoming a Christian, that she began laughing and crying all at the same time. Secrets Julie had kept for years began spilling out.

Julie had been divorced once, before becoming a Christian. Her daughter Meagan was a product of that marriage. Julie moved away from her hometown shortly after the divorce and had little contact with her family. Julie told no one about the second divorce, one live-in boyfriend, and one adulterous affair that had occurred *after* her conversion. Julie was convinced that other Christians didn't commit such horrible sins. Other Christians were perfect. Julie's life was so consumed with guilt that the fear of discovery permeated all her interactions with people. She had no close friends in whom she felt she could confide. Julie's emotions were hovering at the back of her throat like vomit, waiting to be spewed out at the least provocation. She rarely talked to anyone for fear of blurting out her terrible secrets. Julie confided in me for three straight hours; I hardly spoke. A couple of weeks later we began a study on forgiveness and left our sins where they belonged, with God.

Julie soon became an active member of our church and to this day has a vital ministry of helps for people in need, at the church and in the surrounding community.

Guilt is the great American pastime, the universal language. We use guilt as a weapon to force our children to behave and we wield guilt as a club in order to make ourselves step back into line. We also use guilt as an excuse to justify our depression, substance abuse, and even our suicides. What we are *not* doing is using guilt as God intended it to be used, as a gift.

Guilt comes in two packages: legitimate guilt and self-inflicted guilt. Legitimate guilt is a gift from God. God gives this painful emotion to us so that we will stop doing, or thinking, something that is harmful to ourselves or to others.

Let's pretend that you have been gossiping about your "crazy" younger sister, June, with your older sister Kay. This is the one subject that you and Kay can connect with; there is a delicious camaraderie in the "we are so much better than she is" conversations that go on between the two of you. That little fact is tucked away; it's not something you want to dwell on very long. Thinking about it for too long would just make you uncomfortable, and who wants that? Eventually, the Holy Spirit shouts loud enough that you can't help but hear Him tell you that this gossip is a sin. After the next gossip fest with Kay, you feel really terrible about continuing to talk about June. You realize that God had asked you not to gossip again, but you went right ahead and did it anyway. You have been smacked full in the face with your own guilt! You confess to God, determine not to gossip about June again, and call Kay to tell her you are sorry for your part in participating in the gossip. You accept God's forgiveness and move on.

Legitimate guilt was received by you as a gift from God. The sin was confessed, repented from, and restitution was made. God's gift of forgiveness was gladly accepted and gossip was put behind you. Legitimate guilt in action!

I use the letters A-B-C when describing the three types of self-inflicted guilt: Agonizing Guilt, Badgering Guilt, and Contemptible Guilt. We impose these emotions onto ourselves because deep inside we want to somehow "pay" for that thing we did. We are taught from a very early age that bad behavior will be punished. That's the law! If I steal then I will be arrested and probably go to jail. Bad guys get caught, good guys win! However, what if you shop-lift a sweater from your neighborhood boutique? Later, you feel guilty about it so you return the sweater to the store owner. You fully expect a huge lecture, to be banned from the store for life, and maybe the police will be called! Instead, the owner simply says, "Thank you for your honesty. I know this was hard for you. You are forgiven." The shop owner then wraps up the sweater in a beautiful gift box and hands it to you. "Here," she says. "I want you to take this as my gift to you. Next week we are having a big sale on that rack of skirts over there. One of those skirts will look perfect with your new sweater! Please come back then and try one on."

Legitimate guilt in action! You stole, you repented, confessed, made restitution, you were forgiven, and you were invited to come back anytime. That is precisely how we are treated by God after we have confessed our sin. Sadly, many of us won't accept such generosity. For many of us, there is a mean little voice inside our head that will use any opportunity to block the freedom offered by God's forgiveness.

Subconsciously, you think to yourself, "Since the store owner isn't going to punish me, then I guess the only right and just thing to do is to punish myself!" So, you go home repeating over and over again, "What a horrible person I am! What kind of sneaky creep would steal from a nice person like that! I can never face that woman! I will never wear this beautiful sweater she gave me. I can never forgive myself! I don't deserve to be happy. I deserve to feel guilty, forever."

Self-inflicted guilt, plain and simple!

Let me emphasize here that I am *not* saying we do this to ourselves on purpose. Self-inflicted guilt starts in the subconscious. I also don't want to minimize the pain of self-inflicted guilt in any way: the feelings are real, the pain can be excruciating, the suffering is often debilitating. I call this type of guilt "self-inflicted" because it is *not* an emotion that God intended us to have. Once self-inflicted guilt has seeped into our lives, then the beautiful gift of legitimate guilt has turned into a smelly pile of garbage.

I can't say that "I've heard it all" because every story is unique. Each person has his or her own slant on even the most common problem. I am often saddened, but I am no longer shocked, by people's stories. I have learned that human beings are capable of the most vicious cruelty imaginable, but I've also learned that some are capable of surviving horrendous childhoods without inflicting cruelty onto others.

People don't come to talk with me because they feel cheerful and everything is going great. They come because they are in emotional pain. People come to me because they need to tell their own, individual story to someone who will listen without judgment. People talk to me because they want some guidance, some help in getting back onto the path God has chosen for them. People in pain want what we all want: happy families, a sense of fulfillment, and peace with God.

Once I have heard the stories, noted the symptoms, and all the rationalizing has been stripped away; the majority of people I talk to are suffering from guilt.

We sin, we ask forgiveness and then we insist on wearing a crown of thorns, which we press into our own flesh for added pain. Self-inflicted guilt hangs over us like a gray rain cloud, waiting to dump its contents at the slightest incident.

Human beings have a limited capacity for emotional pain. Our brain can only stand so much before we must act out in some way. Guilt can show itself as depression, sadness, crankiness, bitterness, or compulsiveness. We may act out by being overly judgmental of others, being hypercritical of ourselves, rebellious, or we may pretend not to care at all.

Guilt flows through our society like sticky black tar, clinging to and staining everyone it touches. This goop contaminates our marriages, our children, our ministries, and especially our relationship with God.

We must find the way to distinguish between legitimate and self-inflicted guilt. We must find freedom from guilt, in all its forms, forever.

"And the peace of God, which surpasses all comprehension, will guard your hearts and your minds in Christ Jesus." (NASB)

Something to Think About

How often do you find yourself feeling guilty?

Based on what you have read so far, is your guilt "legitimate" or "self-inflicted"? Why?

How do you behave when you feel guilty about something?

Part II: Legitimate Guilt

Chapter Two

Why Would a Loving God Cause Me Pain?

Legitimate Guilt

"If we confess our sins, He is faithful and righteous to forgive us our sins and to cleanse us from all unrighteousness. If we say that we have not sinned, we make Him a liar and His word is not in us." (NASB)

Christina's anxiety attack had occurred in the classroom this time, in front of twenty-two second graders. The room began to close in, sweat poured down her face, and her vision blurred. Chris stood at the blackboard, shaking, trying to remember the answer to the simple addition problem she had written. Her mind was a swirl of disconnected thoughts. Gasping for air, Chris ran from the room to the teacher's lounge where she promptly lost her breakfast.

"Have you had these attacks before?" I asked.

"Yes, but this was the worst. It's never happened in class before, and I've never thrown-up." Christina was of Mexican descent. She was a bi-lingual teacher at a school in a mostly Hispanic neighborhood. Her students adored her, and Chris loved going to work everyday.

"How long has this been going on?"

"It's just been the last few months. I don't know why this is happening to me! Do you think I'm going crazy?" Christina's large brown eyes were pleading for an answer.

"No, I don't think you are going crazy. I think you are reacting to something that is going on in your life by having panic attacks. This is your brain, and your body, telling you that it is time to get something settled. What seems to trigger these attacks?" I said.

"Well, before the classroom thing, I thought being mad at my husband was causing them. Now I'm not sure."

"So, you mostly have these attacks after a fight with your husband?" I asked.

"Not even a fight. Sometimes he just has to be around me for too long. Pretty soon, I can't even stand the sound he makes when he chews! Ray starts bugging me about something, and all of a sudden I've just got to get out of there!"

"Where do you go?"

"Oh, just out. Usually I meet my girlfriend at Lucky's Bar and Grill. We shoot some pool, have some beers. For a couple of hours I can just forget about everything. I even like to pretend I'm someone else."

"Who do you pretend to be?" I asked.

Christina blushed. "Everyone at the bar thinks my name is Maria. They think I'm single."

"Do you act single?"

Chris stirred her coffee. All eye contact was lost during a long pause. "Sort of." She whispered.

"What does 'sort of' mean to you?" I said.

"Well, I guess I do flirt. It makes me feel special, like I'm desirable. Of course, then I feel guilty because I know it's not right."

"Has it ever gone beyond flirting?"

"Only a couple of times. Nothing really happened! We just made out in the corner booth…You know."

"How long have these trips to the bar been going on?"

"Oh, not that long. A few months is all."

"About the same time the anxiety attacks started?"

Chris looked at me for the first time in several minutes. I could see her mind connecting the dots. "Yes…I guess so…Do you think that's what's causing them?"

"Guilt can cause a lot of damage." I said.

Christina's case is a prime example of legitimate guilt. Her behavior was harmful to herself and to others. God kept turning up the heat until she could no longer ignore Him.

Not many people consider guilt a gift. Gifts are usually associated with joy and celebration. It may seem that God is handing us a lump of coal for Christmas when we feel guilty, but that coal will turn into a precious diamond if we will just accept it. The emotional pain from our guilty feelings will transform into peace and freedom once we have taken the steps necessary to seek God's forgiveness.

We are born with the capacity to feel emotion; guilt is an emotion. Feelings of guilt are a gift. I know that sounds strange. If God loves us so much, why would He give us a gift that causes such pain? Because, some behavior is causing harm!

Legitimate guilt is a tool, used to encourage us to stop such behavior and to get back onto the path God has chosen for us. Like a shepherd's staff: guilt nudges, pokes, and sometimes drags us back to the green pastures already prepared for us.

Legitimate guilt is given in love by God and is life-changing. Use this God-given tool to empower your life choices! Guilt is a wonderful, precious emotion that is meant to be short-lived.

On rare occasion, children are born with no ability to feel physical pain. For reasons not yet understood by science, some people's brains do not register the sensation of pain. Many of us might think, "I should be so lucky!" But the truth is, these children who feel no physical pain are in constant danger. A curious two-year-old may see a candle burning and reach out to touch the pretty flame. The sudden pain of getting too close to the heat will cause the toddler to recoil and pull her fingers away from the fire. What if there were no pain associated with that lit candle? Then the baby may grab for the flame and keep her hand there until terrible damage is done.

My father came down with appendicitis and the appendix burst when he was just four years old. If he had not been crying in pain, his parents would have had no way of knowing he was seriously ill. He probably would have died. These children with no pain sensation must be constantly watched and monitored for any sign of physical illness or injury. Many die from an injury or an illness that goes unnoticed for too long. We are built with a capacity to feel pain for a very good reason!

Emotional pain is not always a bad thing. It can be a message from God that we have an internal problem that needs to be faced *now*, so that it won't become a more serious problem later. God gives us the gift of guilt because we have done or thought something that is harmful, offensive, cruel, mean, unlawful or in any way sinful. That can include a long list of deeds, folks! Unfortunately, most of us want to take that gift and form it into a club that we use to beat ourselves up. Some people use guilt to beat themselves literally to death.

Let me give another true, almost comic, illustration of legitimate guilt. A few years ago I was in my local grocery store at the checkout. I had a basket full of items and the clerk was methodically running each item over the scanner. I'm sure she was thinking about what she was going to serve for dinner that night, or the fight she'd just had with her mother; it had been a long day and she was obviously bored. The machine beeped as each item passed; the high school kid at the end of the counter grabbed each one and stuffed it into a bag. As the clerk slid a box of tampons over the glass, I realized that the box hadn't scanned. I had heard no beep and the item didn't appear on the screen. The kid plopped my tampons into the bag and the battle was on!

I felt like a character in one of those "Goofy" cartoons with the angel on one shoulder and the devil on the other. The angel was urging me to tell the clerk about the mistake and the devil was trying to convince me that it was no big deal.

"This store rips people off everyday with inflated prices!" the devil whispered. "It would hold up the line. She'll have to re-check the receipt, unpack the bag to get the tampons, scan the box. The box won't scan because the code will be wrong, so the pimple-faced kid will have to do a price check. Or worse! The clerk will call on the loud speaker, 'Price check on tampons, aisle five!' All for a couple of bucks they're never going to miss in the first place!"

The angel, of course, was reminding me that it was stealing not to tell. You get the picture. The voices got louder and louder as I silently accepted my groceries and drove home. Now the devil, convinced that he had won, was reassuring me that I had done the right thing.

"Don't worry about it! Besides, if you go back now, then they will know that you didn't speak up when you should have; that is as good as admitting to shoplifting!"

By the time I had unpacked the groceries I was wracked with guilt. I decided to work on a lesson I would be teaching for ladies' Bible study. You guessed it…the lesson was on character with an emphasis on honesty! As I read Romans 13: 12-14 for the lesson, my eyes got stuck on verse 13; "Let us walk honestly, as in the day…" I couldn't stand it another minute! I grabbed the tampons and my receipt and headed back to the store.

When I told the clerk that the tampons hadn't scanned and that I wanted to pay for them now, she stared at me like my skin had just turned green. For a full fifteen seconds she didn't move.

The clerk finally snapped back to reality and said, "I'm not sure I know what to do. I've never had a customer come back when the mistake was in their favor."

I told her that I was sorry that I hadn't mentioned it when it happened. I paid, the weight was lifted, and I happily drove home.

The story doesn't end there. After I got home, the little cartoon devil tried another tactic. He wanted me to feel guilty for what I had done even though I had confessed, repented, and made restitution. He started telling me what a terrible Christian I was, that I should have spoken up in the first place. How dare I presume to teach other women a lesson about honesty when I had done such a sneaky thing!

I listened for a few minutes to his lies and then I told him, out loud, to shut up and leave me alone!

I had used the gift of legitimate guilt as it was intended to be used; I had admitted my guilt and then taken appropriate action.

Legitimate guilt arrived because I failed to tell the checker that my tampons hadn't scanned properly. Your legitimate guilt may be caused by something in your past that has gone unconfessed or unrepented. Did you have an affair, an abortion, a shoplifting spree? Are you involved with drugs, gossip, slander, or deceit? Are you holding a grudge against someone, envying them, or thinking that you're better than some other group of people? The list could go on and on; you know what *wrong* means. Is your conscience needling you about some action or thought?

You will receive the gift of legitimate guilt if you have done a wrongful act that has *not* been confessed to and repented from.

Corrie Ten Boom once wrote, "The purpose of being guilty is to bring us to Jesus. Once we are there, then its purpose is finished. If we continue to make ourselves guilty- to blame ourselves- then that is sin in itself."

Legitimate guilt is a signal that the time has come to change a behavior or an attitude that is harmful. Your choice is to confess, repent, make restitution where appropriate, or to run from God and the feelings of guilt. If you choose to confess, then you have opened the gift of guilt and found a wonderful jewel inside the box: forgiveness. No matter what your sin! It's over. Forgiven, forgotten, move on!

Sometimes however, we open that gift and just look longingly at the beautiful jewel of forgiveness. We refuse to take it out of the box and enjoy forgiveness as God intended. We somehow feel that we don't deserve complete forgiveness. We choose to think that what we really deserve is punishment. Now guilt is no longer serving as a gift: guilt has become a curse.

"For I am confident of this very thing, that He who began a good work in you will perfect it until the day of Christ Jesus." (NASB)

Something to Think About

Name some times when you have felt legitimate guilt.

How did you react to legitimate guilt?

Can you look back and thank God for the pain of that guilt?

Is God's forgiveness of that sin enough for you?

Part III: The Curse

Chapter Three

Have I Done This to Myself?

Agonizing Guilt

"I, even I, am the one who wipes out your transgressions for My own sake, and I will not remember your sins." (NASB)

"Twenty years of marriage and Mike just acts like it's no big deal! All I've got to do is sign the papers and it's over!" Carrie sat at the table, wiping her eyes, adding yet another tissue to the pile beside her coffee cup. "It was a disaster from the beginning. It never should have happened. I guess God has been punishing me all these years for what I did."

"What did you do?" I asked.

"I might as well tell you…It will come out eventually anyway….I had an affair with Mike while I was still married to his father. Mike was my step-son. There! I said it! Now you know how terrible I am!"

"You had an affair with your step-son and later married him?" Two decades of experience had taught me not to change my calm tone, but it was a struggle not to react. This was a new one for me!

"Yep! That about covers it!" Carrie chuckled. "Can you get any more stupid than that?"

"Probably not the wisest choice you've ever made." I grinned. "How old was Mike when you started the affair?"

"He was twenty-five, I was thirty-five." Carrie's voice was clipped and matter-of-fact. "Frank, his father, my first husband, was fifteen years older than me. Frank's three children lived with their mother in Seattle when Frank and I married. I had never even met them. Frank and I had been married for ten years when Mike came to Florida to live with us. He wanted to start fresh in a new place, he said. Mike wanted to build up his own landscape business. He loved working outdoors. Mike was young, good looking and full of fun. He even claimed to be a Christian. Everything Frank wasn't."

"Frank wasn't a Christian?"

"No! He wanted nothing to do with God or church. He didn't care if I went to church, but he didn't want to hear about it. Our marriage was pure hell from the start! I guess God was punishing me for that one, too."

"What one?"

"Marrying a non-Christian. I knew better, but Frank was the first man that ever showed an interest in me. After twenty-five years of hearing about what a loser I was from my mother, I jumped at the chance to get married. We were on our honeymoon when Frank informed me he had no intention of ever having more children. I was crushed! I desperately wanted a baby! A few months after we were married he got a vasectomy, just to make sure no 'accidents' happened." Tears began to flow again.

"So ten years later, when Mike showed up, you were pretty miserable." I said.

"That would be an understatement! Within three months, Mike and I were having the affair. I felt guilty and happy at the same time. Both of us thought the perfect solution was for me to divorce Frank so Mike and I could get married as soon as possible. So, that's what I did. The day after the divorce was final, Mike and I got married."

"Were you happy?" I asked.

"At first we were. The day we got married, Mike and I both prayed for God to forgive us for our terrible sin. After praying we truly felt like we could start fresh."

"Did that help?"

"For awhile; but I kept thinking about how sinful the whole thing had been and I would feel guilty all over again. Then I thought if we could move to another state, you know, get away from the bad memories, maybe that would help. So, we moved here to Colorado. I got pregnant with Peggy and I just kept pushing bad thoughts out of my mind. Sure as rain though, eventually in my head I would hear my mother calling me a loser! I wanted to have the perfect marriage, the perfect family, just so I could prove to my mother that she was wrong. That's when I really started fighting with Mike. I was constantly after him about something. After a few years, he just quit trying. Mike started drinking pretty heavy and going out on me. The more I nagged, the worse he got, the worse Mike got, the more I nagged! He quit going to church. Mike said he didn't need some preacher telling him how to live his life, too. Mike blames me for the whole marriage going bad."

"Are you to blame?"

"For some of it yes, but Mike did his share. We are both guilty of this mess."

"Have you asked God to forgive you for your part in the breakdown of your marriage?"

"A hundred times! I pray and pray! But the guilt never really leaves me for long. I feel like there's a hundred-pound weight on my chest most of the time." Carrie burst into tears and another pile of tissue was started.

That session at my dining room table was the first of many more to come as Carrie and I sorted out her tangled web of sin and its natural consequences. Eventually, I was able to help Carrie realize that one of her problems was a large dose of self-inflicted *Agonizing Guilt*.

I call this first curse Agonizing Guilt because this self-inflicted guilt causes us to writhe in pain. We are in agony because this guilt stems from something we really *did* do. The mistake is that we *have already* asked forgiveness, turned away from that sort of behavior, and determined not to do it again. We *are* forgiven by God, but we have not fully accepted that forgiveness. Emotionally we feel the need to be punished, so we inflict this Agonizing Guilt onto ourselves as payment for wrongdoing.

My experience with Bonnie demonstrates the damage that Agonizing Guilt can inflict.

I had been a counselor for fifteen years when Bonnie came into my life. Bonnie was in her early forties, but she looked much older. Forty-plus years of abuse at the hand of others, and by her own hand, had painted her face with deep lines. Bonnie had few memories of any happiness. Twenty years of alcoholism hadn't helped. Bonnie called our church one day in a desperate plea for help. She had been picked up on her second D.U.I. in three years, but this time her seven-year-old daughter had been in the car with her. Bonnie was charged with child endangerment in addition to the drunk-driving charge. She was afraid that the state would take her little girl away from her.

By the time I met with Bonnie, she had not had a drink in four days. Bonnie was jumpy, anxious, sleep-deprived, and unable to concentrate. This was the first time in twenty years she had gone so long without a drink. She laughed about the fact that after her first arrest she would show up at A.A. meetings with a travel mug full of vodka. Bonnie had never experienced withdrawal symptoms before; she was afraid that at any minute she might start seeing pink elephants or start rolling on the floor screaming in a fit of lunacy. I was able to assure Bonnie that her current symptoms were the norm. If the pink elephants hadn't appeared at this point, then they probably were going to stay in the jungle. Bonnie's story unfolded as I met with her weekly. On our third meeting her terrible secret spilled out.

> "I was fifteen, Tony was fourteen. We were playing house. We took care of all the kids while our mothers spent their time at the local tavern." Bonnie smiled at the memory. "We loved each other, we really did. It was the first time either one of us had ever felt love. It never even crossed my mind that I might get pregnant. I had no idea about birth control. Nobody had ever talked to me about such things. Sex was something fun that Tony and I did whenever we had the chance. Our mothers knew we were sleeping together. They never said a word. They were just glad to have someone to look after the little kids, so they could drink all night. I was shocked when I found out I was pregnant." Bonnie's eyes filled with tears and there were long pauses between words as she struggled to control her voice. "The thing is...I was happy about being pregnant. The minute I found out...I loved that baby. I just knew it was a boy. I named him Jacob. I called him Jake when I talked to him. He was Tony's baby and mine. I know it's hard to believe that a fifteen-year-old girl can really be in love, but I was. I was an old fifteen."

Bonnie paused for a long time, twisting the tissue around and around her fingers, swallowing hard and staring at the floor. I urged her to go on. We had come this far; maybe it was time for the whole story to be told.

"I was scared to tell my mom," Bonnie said, "but I finally figured I had to do it because I didn't know what to do next. She and Tony's mom had a fit! They kept telling me over and over that I had to get an abortion. Pretty soon they had Tony convinced, too. I held out as long as I could." Bonnie shuddered and then began to sob, "I cried all the way to the clinic. As long as I live, I will never forget the constant pumping sound of that machine! I could tell when it was sucking blood and when it got hold of my baby. I can still hear it like it happened yesterday! I asked God to forgive me. I swore that very day that no matter what happened I would never have another abortion! I guess God has forgiven me. The Bible says He does, but I can't forgive myself. I murdered my own baby! I will never get over the guilt of that!"

Bonnie's father was a raging alcoholic, with the emphasis on raging. He often held a loaded gun to her mother's head, threatening to blow her brains out in front of the children. When Bonnie was eleven, her mother finally found the courage to leave with the children. In those days, police and local sheriffs were fairly reluctant to step into what they considered "family disputes". Restraining orders were pretty much unheard of, especially in the hills of West Virginia. Bonnie's mother and siblings were often subjected to threatening phone calls, midnight visits, more physical abuse, and filthy language. Bonnie's childhood memories consisted mostly of screaming fights, drunken brawls, and fear. Soon, Mom was bringing "boyfriends" home to live for various lengths of time.

At least Mom did have the sense to throw out the men who hit on Bonnie.

By the time she was fourteen, Bonnie had bounced around among her drunken father, her verbally abusive grandmother, and her now bar-fly mother. Bonnie was trying to find some semblance of family or protection. There was no protection to be found. Anger was Bonnie's frequent emotion and alcohol her only friend. Bonnie was also experimenting with drugs□□, supplied by her nineteen-year-old brother.

Walking home from ninth grade one day, Bonnie accepted a ride from a car full of high school boys. It was a small town, she had a vague acquaintance with the driver. She was gang raped by those five high school boys. Bonnie felt dirty and ashamed. When Bonnie finally got up the courage to tell her mother, Mom told her that the rape happened because she was hanging around with the wrong crowd. Reporting it to the police would only bring shame on the family. Nothing was ever done about the rape.

When she was fifteen, Bonnie's brother invited her to his apartment to get high. After she was thoroughly looped, he demanded sex as payment for the drugs and beer. This time she didn't bother to tell Mom.

Shortly after that night, the Brown family moved next door: a single mother with two pre-school children, and fourteen-year-old Tony. Tony was funny, cute, and kind.

The two mothers became fast friends when they discovered that they frequented the same tavern. Leaving the kids to fend for themselves, the two women walked the short distance to the bar every night around 5:00. Since they were both stuck babysitting, Bonnie and Tony joined forces and set up a household of sorts. They confided in each other and soon sought consolation in sex. Their child was a natural consequence of their actions. Bonnie's first feelings of guilt and horror at having had an abortion came as a gift from God in order to turn her to Him for forgiveness and healing.

I know what some of you are thinking, "But Bonnie *should* feel guilty! That was a terrible thing! Abortion is murder!" I could not agree more. I believe that abortion is murder and that she should have felt guilty. My point is that Bonnie *did* feel guilty. Bonnie begged forgiveness from God, she repented, and she never had another abortion. Bonnie did everything right in the beginning, but unfortunately she then carried guilt a step further. Bonnie refused to forgive herself.

Bonnie's story is a classic example of agonizing guilt; *she did do wrong.* Bonnie then chose not to fully accept the unconditional love and forgiveness that God was holding out to her. Bonnie chose to clothe herself instead in that self-inflicted guilt that tells us we are not allowed to move on with our lives. She could not understand that asking forgiveness from God is enough. Bonnie had gotten the message loud and clear from society, her parents, the media, and a host of others that people must be *punished* for their sins. Since no bolt of lightening came down from heaven, Bonnie decided to punish herself. Instead of allowing herself to grieve the loss of her child, she swallowed her Godly sorrow and felt guilty.

Show me anywhere in the Bible the scripture that admonishes us to confess our sin and then beat ourselves up with guilt for the rest of our lives. Go ahead, look it up, I'll wait…can't find it? Neither can I.

I see scripture that says, "I will remember your sin no more…" "As far as the East is from the West, so far will your sins be …" I read about many people, who did much sinning, who were used by God in wonderful ways. King David is pretty much at the top of that list. Adultery, murder, deceit – David did it all! Yet David was called "a man after God's own heart." Look at Psalm 32: David is literally sick with unconfessed guilt. Guilt eats at his very bones! Once confessed, David is jumping for joy! He feels light and young and free! It took King David awhile, but eventually he got the message and used the gift of guilt as God intended. David bathed himself in God's loving forgiveness and moved on down the path God had prepared for him.

I told Bonnie that guilt was a cancer eating at *her* very bones! Her mind had taken a healthy emotion and allowed it to be turned into a festering, putrid, tumor that was eating at her insides and threatening her whole life. Bonnie had spent years trying to kill the tumor with alcohol and drugs, only to have it grow larger. The gift of guilt had been turned into a curse.

We talked about the fact that as human beings we want to see people pay for the bad things they have done, and we include ourselves in that picture. "You should be *ashamed* of yourself!" is a phrase we all have heard, or spoken, on many occasions. We want to *see* the shame, we want to *see* the groveling that we deem appropriate for the crime. It's only right! But God says that if we will confess our sins, then He will be faithful to forgive our sins. Period!

No groveling required! No scarlet letter on the forehead will be imprinted. We are simply, forgiven.

Subconsciously, here is what we are saying to ourselves when we carry around this agonizing guilt. "If I don't hate myself for the rest of my life for the terrible thing I did, then that means that I'm not *really* sorry. I must hang my head in shame in order to demonstrate my repentance."

Sound familiar? You may not have said those exact words to yourself, but think about it now. Is there some truth to what I am saying? We think that to repent means to feel terribly sorry for something, but it doesn't mean that at all. Repent means to turn away from, to turn your back on that behavior, to walk in a different direction. "Go and sin no more," as Jesus said to the woman caught in the act of adultery.

In no way do I want to imply that a woman can have an abortion, pray for forgiveness, and then happily skip down the road of life without a care. The truth is that once God has gotten a hold of your conscience and convicted you of your sin, your life will be forever changed. Being forgiven by God does not mean forgetting that the sin ever happened. I will talk later about the problem when we say, "I know God has forgiven me; but I just can't forgive myself."

There is a huge difference between Agonizing Guilt and Godly sorrow. 2 Corinthians 7:10 says, "For the sorrow that is according to the will of God produces repentance without regret, leading to salvation; but the sorrow of the world produces death." (NASB) Godly sorrow might be described as that deep, heart-felt sadness that we have sinned against God. The sorrow of having chosen our own way of doing things instead of trusting God's promises to always have the very best planned for our future. By all means allow yourself time to feel that sorrow and regret, but please don't confuse that need to feel sorrowful with the misplaced need to feel guilt.

Godly sorrow brings repentance and a determination to follow God instead of self. Agonizing Guilt brings the death of hope for the future.

We can't carry guilt on the surface for very long. Guilt is too overwhelming and too painful to think about all the time. So we swallow it. We stuff the guilt.

Some people stuff the pain down with food, some swallow it down with drugs or alcohol. Some people cover guilt up with compulsive work habits, or cut themselves, or starve themselves. A few people harm others and, too frequently, some people will depress themselves.

An entire pharmaceutical industry thrives on Agonizing Guilt!

Bonnie eventually realized that she needed to grieve over the death of her baby. Bonnie needed to allow herself to feel the Godly sorrow that *she* had swallowed so many years ago. Bonnie also needed to leave her Agonizing Guilt at the foot of the cross, where it belonged.

"As far as the east is from the west, so far has He removed our transgressions from us." (NASB)

Some Things to Think About

Are you holding onto guilt about something you have already confessed?

Did Jesus die on the cross for all sin; except yours?

Do you find yourself saying, "I know God forgives me, but I just can't forgive myself."?

What is the difference between Godly sorrow and Agonizing Guilt?

Chapter Four

Now I Feel Guilty For Things I *Haven't* Done!

Badgering Guilt

"Be anxious for nothing, but in everything by prayer and supplication with thanksgiving let your requests be made known to God." (NASB)

I looked frantically at the clock on the wall and again at my calendar. Man! I had not factored in what would happen if I had to work overtime. I didn't see that one coming. "O.K., O.K…. you can do this!" I coached myself. "You're two hours behind schedule, so something has to go. Think! You can do this!"

I held my day-timer in front of my face as I raced for my car. "Let's see…pick-up Kim, go to cleaners, grocery store, deposit check, pick-up flyers at printer, drop flyers by church, clean apartment, cook dinner, Jonathan at 7:00." Nope! Not one thing could be dropped: I was just going to have to do it all, only faster!

As I sped down the highway, with my ten-year-old daughter strapped in and holding on to the arm rest for all she was worth, I barked out orders. "O.K! You know your assignment! I'll grab the grocery cart and head toward meats. You run to the other end of the store and get olive oil, mushrooms, and French bread! Got it?"

"Olive oil, mushrooms, French bread! Got it!" Kim barked back with great determination.

"Don't let me down, now! Seconds count! Don't get stuck behind some old lady pushing her cart down the middle of an aisle!"

"No old ladies! Got it!" Kimberly's blue eyes had turned to steel. I knew I could rely on her.

I was a blur of speed and agility as I raced down each aisle, tossing only those items listed into the cart. As I sprinted for the check-out I could hear my petite little girl screaming at a stock-boy. "Olive oil! What aisle? I need it now!"

We screeched into the apartment parking lot at 6:15. Only forty-five minutes before my new boyfriend would arrive for his first dinner at my home! Everything had to be perfect! The apartment was a mess. I had been working a lot of over-time lately. Church activities took up Tuesday, Wednesday, and Thursday evenings. I had recently factored in Jonathan. He lived almost fifty miles away, so Friday night and all day Saturday were mostly dedicated to dating, and to making a good impression. Sunday morning and evening always meant church services. There was very little wiggle room. I had to keep up my titles of Super Career Woman, Super Single Mom, Super Christian, and now, Super Date.

"O.K! While I put the groceries away, you grab anything that doesn't belong in the living room and throw it into your bedroom! He'll never look in there. Then, while I clean the bathroom, you clean out the cat box."

The next thirty minutes looked like a Keystone Cops episode run at fast speed. I was sweeping the kitchen when it hit. Suddenly, my peripheral vision became grey, and stars flashed before my eyes. I slid to the floor, unable to stand any longer. I crawled to the bathroom on my hands and knees to vomit. Surely, I had given myself a stroke! This was it! I was going to die, at age thirty-one, of a stroke! All because I had to prove that I could do it all. What a waste!

I actually felt better after I threw-up. I sat on the spotless bathroom floor and rested; all the while chiding myself for being so foolish. I had set myself up so that I felt guilty if I wasn't reaching some impossible goal of perfection. I called for Kim to bring me a yogurt as I realized that I hadn't taken the time to eat all day. Coffee and cigarettes are not on the food pyramid. By the time Jonathan arrived, I felt much better. I opened the door and informed him that I was taking us all out to dinner. When I told him what had happened, he just shook his head.

"I don't care about your clean apartment or your home-cooked meals. I care about you, Shannon."

I knew all of that; I had just succumbed to temporary insanity. I had served myself a big portion of *Badgering Guilt.*

Badgering Guilt is not as obvious to us as Agonizing Guilt. That subtlety is what makes it so insidious, so harmful, and so difficult to root out. I believe that women suffer from Badgering Guilt more than men.

The everyday life of the "Perfect Woman" is dictated by some unwritten code, which we have created or accepted. We feel we have failed if we give in to the fact that we are limited. Surely, there must be a way that I can do it all! Many of us remember a commercial that was popular a number of years ago by Emeraude perfume; it featured a gorgeous woman holding a frying pan. She strutted around singing, "I can bring home the bacon, fry it up in a pan and when he comes home I make him feel like a man! I am *woman…*"

Women have bought into that message. "As a woman I can do it all, have it all, and still have the time and energy to be a tiger in bed!" Right on, sister! Then as "Super Christian Woman" we add some more "skills" to the list.

Today's Christian woman should be able to bring home the bacon, fry it up in a pan, attend a ladies Bible study, bring meals to the sick, help out with the nursery on Sunday, take the dog to the vet, clean the messy house while dinner is cooking, and just as her husband walks in the door after a hard day at work, she can light the candles at a table set for two while soft music plays in the background. Wouldn't you just **love** to be married to that woman?

I'm exhausted just writing all of that! The advertisements on television, in magazines, and on the radio don't come right out and say it, but we want to believe that perfection is possible. We have received the message loud and clear. The Super Christian Woman never complains, is never exhausted, never thinks bad thoughts, never wants to run away, and never says no. The Proverbs 31 woman is pointed to as the ideal we are all to strive toward. Are you kidding me?

When I first became a Christian, I naively asked an older woman in the church if there were some written material around on how a Christian woman was supposed to act. (Remember now, I was thirty-years-old and when the minister said "Turn your Bibles to John 3:16." I thought he meant page three hundred sixteen.) So, this kind lady said that reading Proverbs 31 would tell me everything I ever needed to know about how to be a good Christian woman.

By verse nineteen I was completely intimidated. I knew that this Old Testament woman was so far out of my league that I had no chance to even approach her standards. Verse fifteen shot me clear out of the water! Anyone who knows me knows that I am *not* a morning person!

My point is that the to-do list never ends. We can never do it all. The Super Christian Woman is imaginary, and yet we feel guilty because we aren't reaching the goal. No such goal exists, because the Super Christian Woman does not exist!

For twenty-five years, Sandy had been totally dedicated to husband and children with little regard for her own wants. We had known each other for ten years, and she had told me on many occasions that she could never really relax. She felt guilty if she wasn't doing something "useful" every minute of the day. Even on family vacations Sandy would quilt blankets for missionaries or, and I'm not kidding, darn socks. "Idle hands are the devil's playground," she would say to herself, or anyone who questioned her compulsive busyness. Sandy was not a happy person, even though she never openly complained.

When the last child left for college, Sandy felt depressed and anxious. She felt like she had lost her personality somewhere along the way. She had been deferring to her families needs and wants for so long that she couldn't even tell me what brand of peanut butter she preferred. Having been motivated by Badgering Guilt in the first place, Sandy even felt guilty that somehow she had not done enough to prepare herself for the empty-nest syndrome the talk-radio hosts had spoken so much about. Sandy's husband sat her down one day and asked her gently if, now that the kids were grown, she could try and find that excited, funny Sandy he had fallen in love with so many years ago.

Sandy and I began months of counseling, centered mostly on expectations. We talked about her expectations of what a good wife and mother "should do" and where those expectations originated. The telling part came when we discussed what she felt other people's expectations were of Christian women in general and of her personally.

"What will people think?" After more than twenty-five years as a lay-counselor, I can tell you that those four words are at the bottom of nearly all the Badgering Guilt that women are carrying around today. We are afraid that *other* people, especially other Christian people, will judge us and declare us to be "not a good Christian," or worse, not a Christian at all. Since these expectations can never really be met, then we display this imaginary perfect behavior at all Christian gatherings.

"If I don't have a spotless house, home-school my children, read only Christian books, give up my career, volunteer for everything at church, read my Bible every day, pray every day, say yes to every request, and speak calmly at all times; then "people" will think that: I'm not a good mother, I'm not a good wife, or I'm not a mature Christian."

Whew! Imagine how it feels to carry all of that inside of your head! Oh, but wait! Most of you reading this book *can* imagine the feeling because you *are* carrying it around in your head. "What will people think, what will people say if I don't put up this front of a perfect home, husband, children, and walk with God?"

Hmmm…isn't that pride? Take away your natural desire to: only want the best for your children, wanting your dear husband to feel good when he comes home at night, and only wanting to serve God. Now, look for the pride of doing it all and the guilt that comes from knowing that you can't keep it up. Aren't you afraid that other people and God won't love you, won't like you, won't approve, if they find out what is *really* going on inside this perfect picture you're trying to create?

Pride sneaks in when we want to keep up the appearance of having it all together. The fear follows because we know that it isn't the truth and that we may be discovered at any time. The guilt badgers us because we insist on believing that *somewhere* that Super Christian Woman *is* doing it all and *having* it all, and so should we.

All humans want to be loved, liked, well thought of; it's part of our human nature. The problems come when we think that what we *do* is what defines us. I fell into that trap, again, myself.

Thirteen years ago I discovered that I had breast cancer. When the doctor called to tell me the news, he asked if we could meet the next day to discuss my options. I looked at my calendar. Literally every space for the next four weeks was filled with at least three things. My husband was a chaplain during that time at a drug and alcohol re-hab farm, and I was running the educational portion of the program for the thirty men. I was also home-schooling our son, teaching a ladies' Bible study at my church, counseling three women, and re-organizing our church library.

Whew! I was the poster child for Badgering Guilt. I was Super Christian Woman to the max! I felt guilty every time I had a minute to myself because I *should be* doing something *useful.* There were not enough hours in the day to complete all the projects I had agreed to be involved in. My calendar said that I didn't have time for cancer; my body said differently. I told my doctor that we could meet the next day; my calendar had just been cleared.

I did *nothing* for the next six months but go to treatments, surgery, and sit on the couch. I lost every hair on my body. I was so anemic that getting up to brush my teeth was a major event. My self-esteem took a nosedive. I looked like a peeled potato and felt like I had been mashed to boot.

One evening while at a restaurant I tearfully confessed to my husband, Jonathan, that I didn't believe he could still love me. I felt useless and ugly. How could such a gorgeous man still love someone who contributed nothing to his, or anyone else's, life? His eyes filled with tears and I could see the pain I had caused by that confession.

"I love you because of who you are, Shannon; not because of what you do or what you look like. If I was in an accident and was paralyzed from the neck down, would you stop loving me?" He asked.

"Of course not!" I said.

"Then how could you think so little of me? Why would you ever believe that I would be so shallow as to love you because of what you can do? I love you because you exist. You are my very life."

Five years ago, breast cancer was back again. I am happy to say that this time around I did not take as big a nosedive as I did the first time. I still lost every hair, I still felt like a mashed boiled potato much of the time, and I felt some depression now and again; but I didn't feel that my self-worth depended on what I could do for others. I felt no urge to over-achieve. I allowed others to help me and I just determined to get through the treatments as peacefully as possible. I discovered that "No." is a complete sentence!

God had used cancer to teach me a very important truth. God loves me simply because I exist! What I can, or cannot, do has no bearing on His love for me. The same goes for all of us. God simply loves us, no strings attached.

After talking to literally hundreds of women on this subject, and after struggling with Badgering Guilt myself, I can assure you that letting go of your guilt and pride is the most freeing thing that can happen. You will find that once you allow the chinks in your armor to show, people will actually warm up to you.

Group therapy works on the principle that people will feel more comfortable, and will be more willing to discuss their problems, if they are with others who have had similar experiences.

Alcoholics Anonymous, for example, allows only alcoholics to sit in on group sessions. Hearing of how another person with the same addiction is learning to cope on a daily basis can bring credibility and comfort. People in the group will admit things to each other that they may not be willing to share with a non-alcoholic. If I am trying to tell someone how hard it has been for me *not to* buy that bottle of vodka I so desperately crave, then I want to say that to a person who has been in the same situation. Someone who has never struggled with alcohol may be sympathetic, but he or she cannot really understand what I am going through. I need to talk to someone who understands how much I really want that drink. That need to seek out people with similar experiences applies to one-on-one relationships as well. I call it being transparent.

Transparent people are far more effective in God's service than those who try to keep up the appearance of perfection. People who are transparent allow others to see into their lives, mistakes included. Once you begin to share your struggles with others, then they will be open with you as well. A bond is formed when that happens. Friendships flourish between transparent people, and lives are changed. Mostly, you will experience the joy, warmth, and unconditional love that God feels for you.

"And the peace of God, which surpasses all comprehension, will guard your hearts and your minds in Christ Jesus." (NASB)

Something to Think About

Do you find it hard to say "No." when asked to do something?

Do you feel you must come up with a "good" excuse as to why you are saying "No."?

Are there any tasks you could remove from your to-do list?

What would people think about you if you said "No." to the next task?

Chapter Five

Is This Guilt or Is This Shame?

Contemptible Guilt

"He heals the brokenhearted, and binds up their wounds."(NASB)

"I was three when they adopted me, the same age their real daughter was when she died." Paula's face was emotionless as she said those telling words.

"Their *real* daughter?" I said.

"Yes, her name was Amanda. I'm told that she was darling, and funny. Smart, too. She was their pride and joy. She died of leukemia. A year later they adopted me. I was supposed to take her place."

"Did they tell you that?"

"No. My brother did. He's six years older than me. Tim never lost an opportunity to point out how different I was from little Mandy. Whenever we fought, he would tell me how Mom and Dad were always talking about what a disappointment I was to them. How I never really fit into the family. How obvious it was that I wasn't a *real* Stromberg."

"That must have hurt. Did you talk to your parents about what he was saying?"

"I tried. Dad accused me of lying. Mom said that Tim would never say such a thing. They said I should be grateful that they adopted me. Look at all the poor kids who never get adopted. That sort of stuff."

"Were you grateful?" I asked.

"No! I was angry. I wished they had adopted someone else. They wanted me to be their dead daughter! I tried my hardest to be what they wanted, especially when I was little. I just wasn't smart enough, or cute enough, or Stromberg enough. I couldn't do anything right. I can't remember them ever saying 'Good job, Paula!' They never said 'I love you.' or even 'We're proud of you.' They made it quite clear that I was a big mistake."

"Did they show any affection to you?"

"Only when someone was watching. Like when Dad had the employees from his bank over for Christmas. Dad might pat me on the back and smile, if someone asked if I was his daughter. Other than that, I can't remember ever being kissed, or hugged, or even talked to very much."

"Did they show affection to your brother?"

"All the time! Tim could do no wrong. His wish was their command. They bought Tim a red sports car for his sixteenth birthday!"

"Wow! What did you get when you turned sixteen?"

"They actually forgot it was my birthday! I kept thinking that any minute they would come out with some big surprise gift, but they never did. A few days later, Mom baked a cake and said she was sorry they forgot. They had been so busy lately."

"Did they give you a present?"

"I got a gift certificate for $75.00 to a bookstore; they were always trying to get me to read. I bought a magazine there and then used the change to buy pot."

"What do you remember feeling during your years at home?"

"Guilt, mostly. Loneliness. I felt guilty because I wasn't smart enough in school. I wasn't coordinated enough to be any good at sports. My dad wanted me to get a scholarship to college, like he did. I was only average. Another proof that I wasn't a *real* Stromberg! I felt guilty that they had chosen me, instead of some other girl that would have made them happy. It was my fault. I wasn't good enough. I didn't deserve their love."

Paula was suffering from guilt and low self-esteem. Through no fault of her own, she had been covered in *Contemptible Guilt*, instead of the love she deserved.

Contemptible Guilt feels dark, confusing, and evil. I hate this kind of guilt with a passion! This guilt is the most difficult to define and the most difficult to banish. I have named it Contemptible Guilt because the victims feel contempt for themselves; also because the actions of the predators are worthy of our contempt. I see Contemptible Guilt most often in the lives of people who have been sexually, physically, or mentally abused as children.

I think of the effects of Contemptible Guilt like touching a corner of porous white paper to a pool of black ink. The black liquid slowly absorbs into the paper. The wettest part of the corner is very dark, but as the ink travels, you can see all the little lines and fibers become tainted with color. Eventually, if the pool of ink is deep enough, the entire sheet of paper will be changed from pure white to various shades of black and grey. By the time the ink has dried, it has become a part of the very fabric of that paper. Contemptible Guilt is like this because blackness seeps into the lives of its victims at a young, impressionable age. Little people find it difficult to understand that *others are imperfect*. Children of abuse are the victims, yet they grow up feeling that *somehow* this crime against them is their fault.

Contemptible Guilt is that persistent feeling of being somehow unclean, of always being wrong, of being unlovable, and of being at fault. Self-hatred is often a companion. A voice in the head is frequently whispering condemnation. These feelings are straight from the pits of hell!

People with Contemptible Guilt live in fear: fear of close relationships, fear of the secret being found out, fear of punishment from God, fear that they are insane, and even a fear of happiness. They often think that if they do experience happiness it will be snatched away because they don't deserve it. What they deserve is misery because they feel that way down deep in their souls. There is a feeling of powerlessness. No matter how smart, cooperative, accomplished, or funny; the child can never change the basic dynamics of a dysfunctional family. There is a feeling of helplessness and hopelessness as well. The attack could not have been stopped. The victim has no time to get help or even make a choice! The opportunity to choose is stolen. There is a sense of being small, helpless, and alone. Shame is just as an effective tool as the threat of bodily harm.*

These innocent victims are drowning in guilt and shame.

Guilt and shame are often used interchangeably. I use the term Contemptible Guilt in this chapter because many people have not recognized that what they are feeling is shame. All bad feelings are just thrown into a bucket of pain labeled "Guilt". I recently attended a conference for Christian counselors. Dr. Richard Shaw was teaching a session on embarrassment, guilt, and shame. His explanation of the difference between guilt and shame was so excellent that I asked his permission to use some of his material in this chapter. He graciously consented. Please visit Dr. Shaw's site at ShameNoMore.com for more information.

Guilt focuses on behaviors and values. It develops later than shame, after the age of three. If a person is capable of experiencing guilt, he has developed some inner rules and a conscience. One can feel badly about behavior but can still respect the self.

"We may feel guilty because we lied to our mothers… (but we) feel shamed because we are not the person our mothers wanted us to be." Smedes (1993)

Guilt is healthy, it helps us do things right; when we need correction, it's there to serve us. Guilt responds proportionately to an event or action.

By contrast, shame is a sense of being completely diminished or insufficient as a person. It is the self-judging the self. The feeling may be so intense that one feels completely bad, inadequate, or unacceptable; devoid of all dignity or worth.

Shame is the inner voice that says we are not good enough, worthy enough, or competent enough. The idea comes from family, friends, or authority figures. Shame is disproportionate to the event or action. A trivial event can trigger a massive feeling of shame. Old shame is triggered by current events or people.

Shame becomes our lens on how we see our life; based on how we think others see us.

Donna has that inner voice of shame so deeply imbedded she can barely function. All of her life Donna has been plagued by eating disorders, drug and alcohol abuse, and debilitating depression. Today she is home bound, on social security disability, living in a filthy house, and heavily medicated. All of this came about because of the sexual abuse she endured at the hands of her own father. It started when she was just two years old.

Donna is the middle child of three children. Their father forced Donna and her two brothers to perform sexual acts on each other while he watched and took pictures. This monster made quite a nice income off the sale of those pictures. Donnas' older brother left home when he was fifteen, never to be heard from again. The younger brother is schizophrenic and spends much of his time between mental institutions and jail. Sadly, Donna feels that her brothers' problems are her fault. She says that as she got older she should have stood up to her father. She should have said "No."

Donna has a young daughter from a failed marriage, so I asked her, "If Linda had come to you and told you that she had been raped by the man next door, would you have told her that it was her fault? That she should have stood up to the man and told him 'No'?"

"Of course not!" she said, "She's just a little girl! She can't be expected to protect herself from a grown man!"

"Then why do you think that you should have been able to protect yourself from your own father whom you loved and trusted? The man sexually abused you for ten straight years. It would have continued longer if your parents hadn't divorced. You were so young when it started; you couldn't have possibly stood up to your father."

Donna stared at me as if I had spoken those words to her in French. She heard my voice, but the concept that she had been an innocent victim was not penetrating her wall of shame.

Donna has been in therapy for her depression for many years; as far as I know, I am still the only person she has told of her terrible history. I have repeatedly encouraged her to tell her psychiatrist, but Donna calmly refuses. She has even endured shock treatments in an effort to stabilize her life. Donnas' psychiatrist simply medicates the symptoms now.

Donnas' case is an extreme result of Contemptible Guilt, but not all that uncommon. I have talked with many, many victims of abuse over the years and most carry this dark shame inside.

I ran a group for victims of abuse a few years ago. I only allowed seven women in the group in order to give enough time for each to share her story. All seven had been sexually abused; two women were now sixty or older. At the fourth session we discussed compulsions. Victims often have compulsive behaviors such as; frequent hand washing, having to check that the door is locked several times before leaving the house, having such things as knick-knacks lined up precisely in a certain position, or having the fringe on a throw-rug perfectly straight at all times. No one wanted to talk about her compulsions. People who suffer from compulsions most often keep them a secret; they think that they are the only ones who do such odd things. They are afraid that others will judge them as insane.

I explained compulsive behavior to the group, and then I asked the women to share. A full ten minutes of silence went by before one brave soul quietly admitted her compulsion.

It seems that every time Pam laundered her sheets, as she took them out of the dryer she had a compulsion to fold them (even the fitted sheets!) exactly the way they had been folded in the package when she first bought them. Each sheet was carefully, precisely, folded as if brand new. This behavior happened even when those same sheets were going to be put directly back on the bed!

There was a moment of silence, and then two more ladies confessed to the exact same compulsion! We had a good laugh, and soon many other compulsions were gleefully confessed. Huge relief was felt as they unburdened themselves by revealing these long-held secrets!

After all my years of lay counseling, I am still saddened at the large number of abuse victims. Abuse knows no boundaries. Children are victimized in every religion, race, economic class, and culture. These little people grow up to be wounded adults who must suffer the consequences of some one else's sick behavior.

Imperfect, trusted, *others* are the people who abuse. Abusers are often people who were abused themselves at a young age. Abusive behavior deserves no excuse. We are all responsible for our own behavior once we have reached a certain age. Sin exists in this world, and innocent people sometimes reap the consequences of someone else's sin. That is not an excuse or a comforting explanation, but it is the truth. The good news is that there are many groups and trained professionals who specialize in treating victims of abuse. There is help available! The *best* news is that God cherishes every cell in our bodies. God is *not* limited, or imperfect! He *is* able to heal our broken spirits.

"A bruised reed He will not break and a dimly burning wick He will not extinguish, He will faithfully bring forth justice." (NASB)

Something to Think About

What are some of the differences between guilt and shame?

Is abuse ever caused by the victim?

Where is the line drawn between discipline and abuse?

Chapter Six

The Big Bucket O' Guilt

Make Mine the Super Size!

"There is therefore now no condemnation to those who are in Christ Jesus, who do not walk according to the flesh, but according to the Spirit." (NKJV)

At this point, I realize that many of you are struggling to put your particular guilt into one of the four categories: Legitimate, Agonizing, Badgering, or Contemptible Guilt. I'm going to throw one more look at guilt in here in an effort to help you see where it hides most often. You will see that the majority of our guilt is badgering us, although the other "guilts" show up now and again. I'll call this The Big Bucket O'Guilt because there is a piece of guilt in this bucket for everybody!

Parental Guilt

This guilt could fill a book all on its own, but I'll touch on some of the more common traps of parental guilt we accept into our lives.

A Disabled Child

Mothers often feel guilty when they give birth to a disabled child. Moms carry this guilt because there are so many unexplained reasons why a baby is born with some sort of disability. Moms feel they must find a logical cause; someone or something to *blame*. Pregnancy books are full of warnings about: what to eat or not to eat, medications to take or not to take, what to drink or not to drink, vitamins to take; also herbal remedies verses standard remedies for pregnancy ills. What music to listen to while pregnant is even given a high priority on the list of "does and don'ts". Disasters will happen if you are too stressed during pregnancy! Be careful about the air you breathe and at what altitude you breathe it!

There is much good advice out there that pregnant women should pay attention to, but there is much silliness as well. I am surprised at times that young women even have the guts to get pregnant! When a woman then gives birth to a child with physical or mental challenges she often will wonder what she did wrong. Could I have prevented this by being more careful about what I ate, drank, listened to, or thought? If only I had known sooner that I was pregnant maybe he wouldn't have been born with these problems. I will talk a little later about guilt during the grieving process, but for now I want to say that guilt stemming from the birth of a disabled child is very common and not from God.

Bonding Guilt

Mothers also may feel guilty because they have never really bonded with a child. We are told by virtually all the movies, books, and magazines that we will feel this great, unconditional love the moment we realize we are pregnant. If we don't feel this love, at least by the time the baby is born, then there is something terribly wrong with us. Also, it is completely taboo to admit that you favor one child over another. Most women who have felt this way will not admit these feelings even to their husbands or closest friends. As a counselor, I hear it more often than you would think.

I was terrified when my daughter was born! I did not feel bonded with her when she was in the womb and I felt no bond for the first few weeks. I needed to get to know her. She was a little person with her own personality. Even though she had been inside me for nine months, she was a stranger to me.

Preferring or being more comfortable with one child over another does not mean you don't love each of them. It simply means that you are more able to relate to one child, probably because of personality. I have lost count of the number of mothers whom have wept bitter tears over their inability to feel a special closeness with one of their children. One mother in particular decided to "make up" for that lack, by giving the "un-favored" child every physical thing he asked for! He quickly caught on and got more outrageous with his demands with each birthday and Christmas request.

To Work or Not To Work Guilt

Working mothers often feel terrible guilt, especially when their young child cries at being dropped off at daycare. The "ideal" Christian mother prefers to stay at home with the children; which is great if you can afford to stay home or if you don't mind giving up a career you love in order to stay home. Reality bites! Many mothers today cannot take the financial hit of staying home. Some mothers will resent having to stay home to raise the kids so much, that the whole family will suffer.

There was a woman in my church many years ago that had been trained as a pharmacist. Eight long years of medical school and many financial sacrifices went into that Doctor of Pharmacy degree! She worked for five years building her business before she became pregnant. Her husband, siblings, parents, and church members all made it clear that the only choice was to give up her career to raise this child. This was the late 1950's and still unusual for a Christian woman to insist on a career. She stayed home for eighteen years and hated her life. Yes, she loved her daughter, but she resented the cage she felt she had been forced into. Her daughter sensed that resentment and they never did have a very close relationship. I'm sad to say that by the time I knew this woman, she was angry and bitter. We need to give ourselves permission to do what we need to do, without the guilt! Go before the Lord with your struggles to work outside the home or to stay at home with the children. Be at peace with the Lord about your decision, which ever way you decide to handle it; but don't let well-meaning family and friends, or society, decide for you.

My Child Isn't Measuring Up Guilt

We all find it difficult not to compare our child with another persons' child. These days it is not politically correct to speak of such comparisons, but we have all done it. If the kid down the street gets a new bike for Christmas and I can only afford a used bike, I feel guilty. I should have been more careful with our finances so that he doesn't have to feel embarrassed about his used bike. If the kid down the street is on the champion soccer team then I feel guilty because I didn't take the time to practice with my child more. Now here's the big one; if my child won't sit quietly in church like the other kids her age, then I feel guilty! (I found it helpful to make up stories in my own head about how terrible those little kids were once they got home!)

My good friend spent many a late night doing her son's book reports, science projects, and math homework. Barb was afraid that if he didn't do well in school the teacher would think poorly of *her*. The thought of someone judging Barbs' performance as a parent brought up all the guilt she carried. Barb felt guilty because she used very poor judgment and had married a terrible man. Barb divorced him before her son was old enough to get the picture of what a creep his father really was. Barb felt guilty because she needed to work, because she often got cross with the boy, and because her son was lazy about school work. Barb got very good grades all through *his* school years. When her son hit college and was on his own; he flunked big time!

Parenting can be one Big Bucket O'Guilt, just waiting to dump on us! The trick is to tell yourself the truth. The truth is that all of us, no matter what our circumstances, can only do the best we know how to do *at the time.* None of us are going to get through parenthood with perfect kids. Comparisons are useless because you will always find some kid smarter, faster, or better behaved than your little darling. Allowing your children to make their own mistakes while still at home is the best way for them to learn. That's life!

Divorce Guilt

Christian society reflects much the same behavior as secular society. We are subject to the same stresses and to many of the same mistakes. Our churches are peppered with people who are already, or will be soon, divorced. I was divorced many years ago and I can tell you that even though I was not a Christian at the time, I still agonized over my decision. Many of my clients have suffered through divorce. I have never met a woman, Christian or not, who took divorce lightly. We feel guilty and the long list of "I should have done…" and the "If only…" is marched out on a regular basis. I should have tried harder! My children are doomed! God hates divorce, so He hates me! I let my whole family down! I can never show my face at church again!

Why do we feel guilty about divorce? Because we have broken a promise, a covenant to live our lives married to that one person. Should we feel guilty? Yes! Then the next step is to pray and ask God's forgiveness for our part in the divorce. Are we forgiven, even as Christians who divorce? Of course! Are the natural consequences of divorce going to cause problems in our lives? Of course!

I do need to put in my two cents here regarding reasons for divorce. There are as many reasons for divorce as there are divorced people. All marriages are unique. But there are some "good", if you can even call them that, reasons for divorce. Abuse of any kind cannot be tolerated! Physical abuse often starts out as demeaning remarks, screaming rages, threats, and controlling behavior. Rape in marriage happens much more often than reported, "No!" means "No!", even in marriage. Verbal abuse is as harmful as physical abuse, but the punches don't show up in public as clearly. Un-repented adultery is most often pointed to as the only "Biblical" reason for divorce. <u>Wishing that you could catch your husband with another woman so you can divorce him and still be in good standing at church, is not a good reason for divorce</u>. It is however, a good reason to drag both your butts to a marriage counselor!

The Bible is clear that "All have sinned and come short of the glory of God." There is no "grading" done by God about which sin is worse than another. Even though we often might say, or think, "I'm bad, but at least I'm not as bad as *she* is!" God does not see one sin as compared to another. Sin is sin; a rose is a rose. Jesus died once, for *all* sin! So, let's not play this game with ourselves about how divorce is the worst sin *ever*. The natural consequences of divorce are far reaching and long lasting; often more so than other sin. However, divorce is still forgiven and remembered no more by God.

Financial Guilt

"Money is the root of all evil!" How often have we heard that verse quoted?…Oops! I meant *misquoted*. 2 Timothy 6:10 says , "For the *love* of money is a root of all *sorts* of evil…" (NASB). Financial problems are often our secret little guilt because we don't have the nerve to talk about our debt to anyone. Especially not someone at church!

God does not want me to ever have debt, because that is not being a "good steward".

I have, over the years, personally known a number of Christians who have managed to get through life with no debt, except for their house. I invariably feel guilty around these very sincere people. Just a few months ago a middle-aged couple at our table in Sunday School remarked that the last of their three children was about to leave for college. They were feeling very pleased that the goal of not incurring *any* debt while still being able to handle tuition, had been reached. Congratulations and a small smattering of applause followed. I was happy for them; and embarrassed for me. I'm pretty sure I was not the only one in the room feeling those mixed emotions.

Good Christians do not have debt? I have a problem with telling myself that lie. Because, you see, I *am* a good Christian and I *do* have debt. I am a born-again-Bible-thumping-Christian and I have debt. Plenty of debt! As a matter of fact, I would be happy to give you some of mine if you are feeling left out in the whole debt thing! Poor planning, impulse buying, unemployment, the national economy, and stupidity have all contributed over the years. That horse left the barn a long time ago! So, is feeling guilty about my debt going to help in any way? Only to the extent that I prayed for forgiveness for my part in it and have tried diligently not to repeat the same mistakes. Once I have confessed and repented, I need to move on.

In today's economy it is very difficult to avoid debt. I applaud those of you who have managed to stay debt free! But for those of us who do carry a burden of debt, guilt is not going to shrink that debt even one dollar. Confess that impulse purchase, determine not to fall into that trap again, return the item if possible, and move on. Cut your credit cards up as you pay them off and then shred them. Throw away those glossy sale catalogues you get every week without so much as a glance. For heavens' sake, don't ever turn to the shopping network! There are many things that we can all do to mend our bad spending habits, but feeling guilty is not one of them.

One more thing about spending habits; if you have an urge to go shopping every time you feel "down", then you may be suffering from depression. Ask yourself these questions: When I am angry or sad does a shopping spree make me feel better for a little while? Do I consistently find myself spending more than I should? Is my closet stuffed with clothes I hardly wear or things I never use? Does my spending cause problems at home? If you can answer yes to any of these questions then it would be a very good thing to talk to your doctor about it. Depression can show itself in many forms and compulsive spending is a very common symptom.

Body Image Guilt

If you have *never* looked in a full-length mirror while trying on a bathing suit and wanted to punish yourself for eating all that fast food, then go ahead and skip this guilt. The truth is, most of us have wasted countless hours haranguing ourselves for allowing that extra weight to creep onto our thighs while we weren't paying attention. There is often a vicious cycle of guilt for having eaten a sleeve of mint cookies for lunch rather than the garden salad with fat-free dressing we had intended; then that makes us feel down so we eat French fries to soothe our pain. "I've already blown it, I might as well eat what I want today and start fresh tomorrow." is the dieters' mantra. We feel guilty because we have broken yet another promise we made to get that weight off. We feel guilty because we are so undisciplined when it comes to food. We call ourselves lazy, fat, and worse. Honestly, none of the name calling helps. None of the guilt helps. The truth is, this guilt is not from God. The truth is, *God would never talk to you in that tone of voice!* There are currently 24,000 "diet" books in print that will help you to lose weight, but the truth is, losing weight is hard work and keeping it off takes a lifestyle change; not a crash diet.

Our society seems obsessed with weight and with "beauty", whatever *that* is. The tabloids are full of the latest news about which female star; (weight is almost never an issue with male stars) has lost too much weight or gained too many pounds, who needs a face lift or who just had a face lift. Hair color is changed as often as socks! Teenaged girls are going under the knife to have breast implants! The outward appearance seems to be the highest priority these days. Guilt sticks like bubble gum on hot pavement to women who buy into this mass media frenzy. Allowing some faceless fashion editor to dictate how we feel about ourselves seems absurd, yet we allow it to happen.

Ahhh…there's the rub! **We allow it!**

Grieving and Guilt

In her 1969 book *On Death and Dying,* Elizabeth Kubler-Ross voiced the five stages of grief: denial, anger, bargaining, depression, and acceptance. Her studies were centered mostly on people who were told that they were in the dying process. What has been shown over the last forty years is that the grieving process manifests itself in a variety of circumstances. People grieve: the loss of a job, loss of freedom, death of a pet, loss of ones youthful dreams (often described as a mid-life crisis), suicide of a loved one, loss of innocence, and the loss of the healthy child you expected to be born (as in the case of the birth of a disabled child). Life is actually full of grief! I would like to add one more stage to the list that Kubler-Ross spoke of; guilt.

Suicide

In 1974, I was living in Japan when I received an envelope from the parents of a girl who had been my best friend in Junior High. We both had moved many times over the years, but we kept in infrequent touch. The envelope simply contained the newspaper clipping describing the suicide death of my friend and the subsequent suicide of her lover. I was devastated! I felt as if someone had just ripped my heart out! Within a few hours, I began to feel guilty. If only I had taken the time to call her when I had visited the States a few months before, maybe she would have told me what was bothering her and we could have talked it out. If only I had written her more often, maybe she would have confided what was going on in her life and not gotten so depressed. If only I… The "if only" list was endless. The truth is, there was nothing I could have done at the time. The truth is, she was responsible for her decision to take her own life. The truth is, that even people who only have a mild acquaintance with the person who commits suicide often feel some guilt.

Disabled Child

Women who have given birth to a disabled child often feel guilty, as I mentioned earlier. These parents need to grieve the loss of the healthy child they expected and hoped to give birth to. That does not mean in any way that the mother will love her disabled child any less; it simply means that it is ok to grieve and grief naturally can bring some pangs of guilt. Eventually, these guilt feelings should pass on their own; if they do not pass then meeting with a grief counselor would be a good idea.

Death of a Pet

My online advice column, www.guiltlady.com, receives many guilt concerns, especially over the holidays, about the death of beloved pets. We can get very attached to our pets and so when they pass, the grief is very real. The guilt ranges from "I should have been more careful when I took out the trash because Fido dashed through my legs and got hit by a car!" to "I should have realized earlier that Fluffy wasn't feeling well, she has untreatable cancer!" Although usually shorter in duration, the pain and guilt over the death of an animal can be as traumatic as the death of a human loved one. Please remember my beloved reader that pets are not human beings, even though we too often insist on assigning human traits to them. Take the time you need to grieve the death and then move on.

Amputation

In 1996 I had both my breasts amputated. It was never called an amputation by my doctors or nurses, but that is exactly what it was. Most of us have heard of the "phantom pains" experienced by amputees. A soldier who has lost an arm may feel pain or even an itch in the arm that is completely gone. Well, women who have had one or both breasts removed feel the same thing. I even had that tingling sensation I used to get in my nipples when I was breast feeding and my milk was about to let down! My youngest child was thirteen-years-old when I came down with cancer, so my breast feeding days were long behind me; but I felt that tingle all the same. I still would make the same decision to have a bi-lateral mastectomy (breast amputation) today, but along with the grief came the guilt. My guilt was not rational, it made no sense. Guilt is often irrational. I felt guilty that I had not gone to the doctor sooner, caught the cancer earlier. I felt guilty that my husband was denied the pleasure of sex with a wife who still had all her body parts. I even went through guilt because I had put my friends and family through so much worry and stress with my cancer diagnosis! Amputees must grieve the loss of a body part as well as the loss of function that naturally accompanies that sort of surgery.

Job Loss

Shock and guilt are both strong emotions when it comes to the loss of a job, or even the loss of a promotion you thought sure was just around the corner. Sadly, in today's economy many of us have experienced the various stages of grief through job loss. When the boss calls you in and tells you that your services are no longer required, there is often a big "What?" that shoots out of your mouth before you can stop it. Disbelief, confusion, promising to do better, to work for less, this can't be happening, what am I going to do, anger, and finally, as they escort you out the door, acceptance. By the time you get home the guilt has hit you right between the eyes. "I should have seen this coming, I should have taken that job with the other company when I had the chance, I shouldn't have taken so much sick leave…" Pay attention to any mistakes you could have avoided and move on to the next job. Guilt can cripple your job search if you allow it into your life.

The stages of grief are normal and very real. Not everyone will experience all six, and the stages come and go in no particular order. Grief is a process; not something you can race through in order to finally reach the end and feel all better. You never "get over" a death, an amputation, or a divorce. But you will learn to live through it. You will always live your life differently than if it had never happened, but with God's help your life can be fulfilling and happy again.

Survivors Guilt

My generation went through the Vietnam War, this generation of young men and women are fighting in the Middle East. War does more damage to the heart than to the body, I fear. Scores of soldiers feel guilty because the buddy next to them was killed and somehow they survived. I've known women who survived sexual abuse and felt guilty because some other victim of the perpetrator could not survive; a mother who feels guilty every time she has fun with her children after the death of their sibling. Survivors often feel that it should have been they that died instead; the person who died didn't "deserve to die". I'm the one who should have died. I'm the one who should have been laid off. I'm the one who should have gotten cancer. The truth is we are looking for someone to blame. We are looking for a reasonable answer to our question of "Why". Again, guilt is a normal emotion here but if it persists please seek the help of a counselor.

Green Guilt

Rather than list out all the guilt going around the country concerning global warming and pollution, I'll just take a few pages from my own list of "green guilts". I grew up in the fifties when littering was a way of life. I clearly remember throwing soda cans and fast-food wrappers out the car windows as we careened down the highway at a blazing forty miles per hour. Both of my parents smoked and there was never a thought about what they were doing to our little lungs as they puffed away in the car and at home. Smog was only talked about in terms of Los Angeles. We needed never to worry about such things because that was far, far away in California; and only crazy people lived in Los Angeles. Raw sewage was routinely dumped into Seattle's Lake Washington, but there was nothing to worry about because it was such a huge lake that we would never notice. It wasn't until around 1960 that Woodsy Owl came onto television to say "Hey kids! Give a hoot; don't pollute!" To this day I still hear and see that commercial when I accidentally drop a gum wrapper on the ground and hesitate to pick it up! This whole movement to clean up the environment is a relatively new idea in the whole scheme of things.

So here I am, at my advanced age, feeling guilty because I use too much hot water when I take a shower, I find it nearly impossible to toss a piece of plastic in the garbage, but I would secretly love to own a Hummer. I've pretty much given up fast-food, canned food, and Chilean bass. I re-cycle anything that doesn't run faster than I do. But, age does have its privileges (and quirks). I now live in Virginia. When it is hot and humid in the summer I run my air conditioning all day and night. When it is cold in the winter I turn up the heat. My days of camping in a tent were bid a fond farewell in 1996 while shivering on the side of some mountain in Colorado while a raccoon, whom we were convinced was a bear, rifled through our food box. At 2:00am as we were shoving our rain-soaked camping gear into our car, I screamed to my adult daughter "I am old enough and rich enough to never have to camp again! The next time you want us all to go camping together as a family I will be sleeping at the nearest hotel that has a hot tub!" I feel no guilt for that. I have given in to eating mostly organically grown foods, but I simply cannot stand the taste of farm-fresh eggs or free-range turkey. I think they have too much flavor for me, to tell you the truth. I actually prefer the store-bought eggs that have been in storage for six months and the relatively tasteless turkey they present to us at Thanksgiving. I have a sneaking suspicion that I am not the only one out there with these "anti-green" tastes.

Ridiculous Guilt

One more "soap box", then we're done. Why do so many Christians think that coming right out and saying what their Spiritual gift is would be bragging? Why can't we just take the compliment when someone thanks us for exercising our Spiritual gift? Instead, we blush, look away and tell them "It was nothing." Isn't that insulting to our Lord?

If my husband spends a whole day braving the mall to find me just the right birthday sweater, is it nice for me to refuse a compliment from someone when I wear it in public? If my friend says, "Wow! What a beautiful sweater, it really looks great on you!" Am I supposed to reply, "What? This old thing? It's nothing, I just wore it because I had nothing else to wear today." How would my husband feel about the gift he had given me so lovingly?

Please! Let's stop with the false modesty. Exercise your Spiritual gifts with gusto and joy! When the subject of Spiritual gifts comes up in conversation, proclaim yours happily and thank God for His generosity!

So, I conclude the "Big Bucket O'Guilt" with these thoughts. We all have done things that we should feel guilty about in our lives. Guilt is a legitimate emotion that we need to feel when we have done something that is harmful to ourselves or to another person. But let's get off the guilt band wagon and stop beating ourselves up over things we have already confessed and repented. At the end of the day look back at what has transpired. What, if anything, would you change given the opportunity? Learn from your mistakes and move toward a better day tomorrow. In other words; give yourself a break!

"…For the mouth speaks out of that which fills the heart." (NASB)

Something to Think About

Name the various "guilts" you have been carrying around in your bucket.

Are any of the above "guilts" legitimate? If so, then confess and repent right now.

Do you see a common theme to your self-inflicted guilt?

Part IV: The Cure

Chapter 7

Show Me the Steps Already!

The End of Legitimate Guilt

"And I will restore to you the years that the locust hath eaten,…" (KJV)

The cure for guilt may seem obvious to some people. "Get over it and move on!" I wish letting go of guilt was that simple, but the truth is that any guilt, whether legitimate or self-inflicted, is painful. We feel sad. We must be allowed to grieve. We need to grieve the wrongs that we really have committed. We need to mourn the loss of the time and effort we wasted going our own way instead of following God's plan. We need to take the time to name our guilt and to decide if we are willing to give up the prison of guilt for the freedom of God's path for our lives. Does that sound like a "no brainer"? Wouldn't *anyone* jump at the chance to be free of guilt? Not everyone. Constant guilt breeds its own sense of comfort if you live with it long enough. We need to mourn the loss of the familiar way of life we give up when we let go of our self-inflicted guilt.

Have you spent most of your life trying to please people? Do you think of yourself as dirt? Is anger hovering at the base of your throat, waiting to spew poison at the next person who ticks you off? Are you afraid the *secret* will come out? Are you stuffing your feelings with drugs, alcohol, or food? That behavior, those thoughts, seem normal and right to you. Even bad habits have a level of comfort because they are familiar.

We talk to ourselves all day long, even in our sleep. Think of that conversation as a tape recording constantly running in your brain. We make decisions based on that dialogue. Some of those tapes are ancient and full of bad advice. If you tell a young child long enough that she is stupid, then eventually she will believe it and act accordingly. Even a brilliant child will do poorly in school if she *thinks* that she is stupid. We've all heard the saying about computers, "Garbage in...garbage out." The same holds true for our minds. You have to stop the hurtful chatter!

Changing the tapes in your head will seem awkward and wrong at first. You will want to return to the guilt because guilt is more familiar, and some comfort comes with familiarity. You are *not* going to just wake up the day after reading this book and suddenly feel that all the guilt you have been carrying for years is gone forever, never to return. Relapses are normal, but God will always guide you through the rough times.

Use the gift of guilt as intended by the Giver. Your guilt is legitimate if you have been, or are currently, engaged in some mental or physical activity that is harmful to you or to another being. You are *supposed* to feel so uncomfortable that your strong-will eventually gives in, and you surrender that activity to God. God has provided a way out of this cycle of pain and guilt.

Here are the steps you can take to stop that merry-go-round you have been stuck on for so long:

1. **Stop** the murder, drugs, pornography, excessive alcohol, lying, cheating, gossip, greed, pride, judging, or whatever else you know to be wrong. This may seem like a "no brainer" too, but some of us need to be reminded of the obvious from time to time. What if stopping means giving up a long held addiction? Not so easy an assignment now, is it. What if you are an alcoholic? You prayed three days ago through all of these steps, and really meant it at the time, but yesterday you slipped; you got drunk. Does this mean that it "didn't take"? No. Relapse is an unfortunate part of any recovery. The key here is not to lose heart. Don't tell yourself that "I've blown it now! I might as well just keep drinking.

This is too hard for me. God won't help me anymore." Those are typical lies, straight from Satan. God meets us each day exactly where we are. His love and His help never ceases. Tell yourself the truth. The truth is; you messed up. The truth is; you can turn your back on that addiction. The truth is; there are many people out there who are willing to help you through each day until you can stand on your own. Then you can help some one else. Look forward, not backward. Also, stopping and confessing are often simultaneous; so don't get hung up on the order of the first two steps.

2. ***Confess*** to God. The word translated into English in the Bible as confess comes from the original Greek word <u>homolegeo</u>, which means to speak the same, to agree, to acknowledge or admit. God wants you to *agree* with Him that what you have been doing is wrong. He tells us to confess because confession is something that *we* need, not something *He* needs to hear. God is almighty; it isn't as if He didn't know you were having that affair. He knew it would happen before you were born! You haven't been "getting away with" anything. God knows that if you actually admit your sin to Him, then it will become more real to you, and your pride will step aside long enough for you to be repentant. Now here is the hard part. God tells us to confess our sins one to another.

Yikes! Why would He want us to do such an embarrassing thing? Because God knows us better than we know ourselves. He knows that if we just confess these things silently to Him, then we will use our little tricks to rationalize, excuse, blame, and not take full responsibility for our own actions. Saying the words out loud helps us to see them in full light. Confession also makes us accountable to another human. Confession gives that other person the right to ask later how we have been doing. Some people find it easier to write it out first and then, with a trusted friend in the room, read it out loud to God as a prayer. Confession naturally leads to repentance.

3. **Repent** of your sins. The word repent is used many times in the New Testament. The original Greek words were most often <u>epistrepho</u>, to turn around, and <u>metanoia,</u> to have a change of mind. The English word "repent" does include feelings of sorrow or to be contrite. I have never known anyone who did *not* feel contrition or sorrow after confessing sin, but we need to stop at regret. There is no requirement to feel guilty for the rest of our lives. When the Bible tells us to repent, we are to turn away from that sinful activity and change our way of thinking. Repent does *not* mean to beat yourself up for, to pull your hair out, or to think ugly thoughts about yourself. The idea here is to stop the harmful activity, and to do what it takes to walk away from it.

Repentance may mean that you have to move out of your neighborhood in order to avoid the "friends" that you have been partying with. Repentance may mean that you take a different route home from work, in order to avoid the favorite bar where you used to hang out. It may mean that you are brave enough to tell your gossip buddy that you won't listen to his or her latest stories anymore. Repentance may mean staying home alone on a Saturday night, so you won't be tempted to go to bed with the next cutie pie that comes along. It will also mean not answering the phone calls or emails from your lover. Examine your behaviors, and then figure out how to turn your back on the bad ones. Once you have confessed and repented, then restitution may be in order.

4. **Make restitution**, if appropriate. Jewish law did say that if you cheated some one, then you must pay back four times the worth. Exodus 22 gives clear guidelines for making restitution for a variety of wrongs. Restitution was an acknowledgment or expression of regret. The restitution was to be made *before* a sin offering could be presented to God.

The New Testament provides no legal or ritual application to the Old Testament law, but restitution is clearly pictured in Matthew 5:21-26. Luke 19:1-10 gives an example of restitution in the story of Zacchaeus. Have you stolen or cheated? Pay it back. Have you gossiped about or hated some one? Apologize and ask forgiveness of the person you have harmed, if appropriate. I have written "if appropriate" twice now, because some caution must be observed here.

Many years ago, I received a phone call from a young woman who confessed to me that she had been jealous of me and had hated me for years. She asked my forgiveness. I was stunned! I had no indications of her bad feelings toward me. I told her that I forgave her, but from then on I felt awkward around her. The phone call may have helped her, but it hurt me. I would suggest seeking the counsel of a mature Christian before you approach the person you have wronged. Sometimes the kinder thing to do is to just pray through the Holy Spirit that healing will take place, and leave it at that. However, restitution must be made when it *is* appropriate.

I am saddened to admit that I have hated my ex-brother-in-law. I never did like Dave, and when his jerky behavior began hurting my sister, my contempt grew. I was judgmental and critical of him from the beginning. Dave accused me of having a wrong attitude toward him on many occasions, which I denied. I tolerated his presence at family gatherings and had convinced myself that my attitude did not show, but it did.

I had prayed privately on many occasions over the years, asking the Lord to forgive me for my hateful thoughts. I felt relief after each prayer, but as soon as I would hear of another hurtful act on Dave's part, the old resentments returned full force. It seemed to me that I would never be able to free myself from the cycle of resentments and guilt.

A few years ago, I attended a retreat designed to take people through the steps of forgiveness. I was assigned, as a counselor, two women whom I was to guide through the steps. During my session with one of the ladies it became clear to me that I needed to confess my feelings toward Dave. He and my sister had been divorced for several years by then so Dave and I had little contact. I prayed out loud telling the Lord that I forgave Dave for his hurtful acts, and I, again, asked forgiveness for my judgmental and critical attitude toward Dave. The Lord immediately began reminding me that I had not yet made restitution. "Oh, no! Anybody but Dave, Lord! Don't tell me to call Dave to ask his forgiveness! I'm sure that it wouldn't be appropriate in this case!"

The Holy Spirit would not let it go. He continued to nudge me in the direction of that dreaded phone call. As I headed home from the retreat, the lady who heard my confession asked me what I was going to do. I knew that restitution must be made. We have a saying in our family, "If ya gotta eat frogs, eat the biggest frog first!" As soon as I got home I wrote out what I needed to say, picked up the phone, and called Dave.

"Dave, this is Shannon. Through prayer, the Lord has convicted me of my need to ask your forgiveness for my judgmental and critical attitude toward you all these years. I sincerely apologize and ask you to forgive me. I hope that in the future, we can have a respectful and peaceful relationship with each other."

I was ready for Dave to start shouting, "I told you so!" I was prepared to endure a long list of grievances that Dave had against me. Thanks be to God, that is not what happened! Dave was clearly touched as he said, "Wow! First of all, let me say that I do forgive you. Secondly, I want to say thank you. I know how hard it must have been for you to call me today." We then had a pleasant conversation about his kids and got off the phone.

God had honored my obedience by preparing Dave to be gracious. I felt like a ten- pound boulder had been removed from the pit of my stomach!

Sure enough, a couple of weeks later, Dave did another jerky thing. My sister could not wait to call and tell me the story! I listened and agreed that his actions were wrong but I did not engage in the usual verbal dismemberment of Dave as a person. The great part is that once I got off the phone I realized that the boulder of resentment had not returned. The old feelings were gone! I was free! I could truly move on.

Four "little" steps that can change your life forever. The longer you have been engaging in your sin, the harder it will be to go through those steps but the bigger the pay-off. Once you have cleaned out that rat's nest of sins you will find it easier and easier to stop, confess, repent, and make restitution as new sin crops up. Yes, new sin will crop up! It always does. Satan is not going to take this new you laying down. He will find new, more clever, ways to tempt you to sin. It is your job to keep your mind stayed on the Lord so that you can recognize your own sin and the temptations thrown in your path. Every day!

Now let's look at the steps to rid your life of self-inflicted guilt.

"If we confess our sins, He is faithful and just to forgive us our sins, and to cleanse us from all unrighteousness." (KJV)

Something To Think About

Do you have some un-confessed sin that you have been holding onto? Write it down.

What person can you trust to tell this secret to and will that person keep you accountable?

Is restitution appropriate in this case? Ask God to tell you what, if anything, you need to do.

Chapter 8

What About Self-Inflicted Guilt?

Is There Really an End in Sight?

"Who is a God like Thee, who pardons iniquity and passes over the rebellious act of the remnant of His possession? He does not retain His anger forever, because He delights in unchanging love".(NKJ)

But what about the curse of Agonizing, Badgering, or Contemptible guilt that has been plaguing you for years? How do you rid yourself of that? Let's look at the next six steps:

5. ***Examine your guilt.*** Listen to the tapes running in your head. Think about what it is you have been feeling. Ask yourself the question, "Is this the truth? Does God require that I suffer?" Is this guilt you are carrying helpful to anyone? If this guilt is not helping you to grow spiritually, then it is not from God. If your guilt is not from God, then it is either self-inflicted or from Satan. Either way, it is trash.

Agonizing Guilt can be difficult to leave behind because it stems from something that actually did happen. The old tapes tell us that we *need* to be punished for this terrible wrong. I counsel my clients to take the time to carefully listen to what they are telling themselves. Those hateful, hurtful things you are saying to yourself are not the truth. The truth is; you made a mistake. The truth is; you have confessed, repented, and made restitution. The truth is; the slate has been wiped clean as far as God is concerned. The truth is; **God would never speak to you in that tone of voice!** The truth is; it is time to leave the past behind.

God says that your sins, no matter what they may be, are forgiven. They are erased, they are gone!

Are you badgering yourself to be the Extreme Christian Woman? Ask the question, "What is the truth about all these things I think I *should be doing?*" As Christians we are held to a higher standard to be sure, but God has made even that a reachable goal. Micah 6:7-8 says, "…Shall I give my first-born for my transgression, the fruit of my body for the sin of my soul? He hath shown thee, O man, what is good; and what doth the Lord require of thee, but to do justly, and to love mercy, and to walk humbly with thy God?" (KJV) As far as I can see, no mention is made about a perfectly clean house, being at the church every time the doors are open, never saying no to a request, being a doormat, getting straight A's, never having an unkind thought or harsh word, or any of the other endless ideals that we impose on ourselves. You are human, you are flawed, and no one understands that better than God Himself. He created you for a purpose. God has a path that He wants you to walk with your own unique gifts. God loves you with all of His heart, even if you never do another thing the rest of your life. Now *that's* the truth!

What is the cure for Contemptible Guilt? If you suffer from those symptoms I described, then the cure is much the same as for Agonizing and Badgering Guilt, but with a little addition:

Listen to those tapes running in your head. Where did those thoughts come from? Can you point to some trauma in your life such as sexual assault, mental abuse as a child, or physical abuse? Are there large blocks of your childhood that you can't remember at all? If you can agree that there may be some problem here, then I strongly suggest counseling with a professional who specializes in abuse. Bringing up past trauma is painful, but once the evil can be examined and talked about it will lose its hold on you. You do not have to suffer your entire life. **The abuse was**

not your fault! Freedom from your past is possible. God promises to hold onto you through the entire process. You will never be alone. Reading Dan Allender's *The Wounded Heart* is a good place to start.

No matter which self-inflicted guilt you carry, follow the next four steps:

6. ***Pray against self-inflicted guilt.*** Our strongest weapon against the schemes of the devil is prayer. If you have been beating yourself up with guilt, then Satan has had his hand in it. Ask God to show you where this guilt has been coming from, and then ask for His wisdom in dealing with it. He has promised us wisdom, if we will only ask. Prayer is an intimate conversation with God. There is no special formula to follow, no perfect words that must be said. Open your heart to God; He totally understands what you are trying to say.

7. ***Repent from self-inflicted guilt.*** Turn your back on those guilt feelings. Erase the lies you have been telling yourself for years and replace the lies with truth. Try some of these truths: I am completely forgiven. God loves me for who I am, not for what I do. Any abuse I suffered as a child was because of the sin of another person, not because of something I did. Turn your face away from the past darkness of guilt and look toward your bright future of peace with God. You have the right to be free from guilt.

8. ***Thank God.*** Breathe in your new freedom from guilt. Do you feel lighter? Younger? Relieved? God's forgiveness is the reason. It has always been available to you and it always will be available. Our Lord and Savior, Jesus Christ paid the debt for that forgiveness. Thank Him for His loving gift.

9. ***Forgive your enemies.*** When someone has wounded us deeply, in a sense, a debt is owed. The King James Version of the Lord's Prayer says, "…and forgive us our debts as we forgive our debtors…." As

Christians, we know that Christ paid the debt that we owed to God for all of our sins: past, present, and future. We accept that we must continue to ask forgiveness for current sins in order to keep the path of our relationship with God cleared of obstacles. The sticky part comes when God asks us to forgive our enemies. More on forgiveness later.

10*. Move on*! Once you have taken care of this matter with God it is over, a done deal. In 1972, *Guideposts Magazine* carried an article written by Corrie ten Boom entitled <u>Love Your Enemies</u>. In that article she wrote, "When we confess our sins," I said, "God casts them into the deepest ocean, gone forever. And even though I can't find a scripture for it, I believe God then places a sign out there that says, 'No Fishing Allowed.'"

The gift of guilt has been used as it was intended to be used, so don't allow yourself to pick that guilt back up and use it as a curse. I am not saying forget it and move on. "All have sinned and come short of the glory of God." We all have done things we deeply regret. No woman is going to forget the abortion she had. We are human beings and we will remember the sins we have committed throughout our lives. But also remember this; your penalty has already been paid. There is an old hymn that says; "Jesus paid it all, all to Him I owe. Sin had left a crimson stain, He washed it white as snow." That sin is forgiven, over, gone, forgotten. God says, "…and I will not remember your sins." Tell yourself *that truth*; everyday if you have to!

"As far as the east is from the west, so far hath He removed our transgressions from us." (KJV)

Something To Think About

Take some time to listen to that voice inside your head. What are you telling yourself?

What seems to be the main theme in the lies you are telling yourself?

Where did those lies come from?

What is the truth?

Part V: The Final Road To Freedom

Chapter 9

Forgive My Enemies?!

Forgiveness; The Hard and the Very Hard

"When you begin a journey of revenge, start by digging two graves; one for your enemy and one for yourself." (Chinese Proverb)

An entire chapter is given to forgiveness because it is so vital that you understand what forgiveness truly is, and what forgiveness is not. I want you to understand that forgiveness will empower you to kick free of the last shackles of guilt.

I want to address one of the most problematic issues of forgiveness first. Here is what I hear from women far too often; "I know God forgives me…but I can't forgive myself!"

I can fully understand the sentiment behind that statement, but Biblically, it's completely screwed up. If God Almighty has seen fit to forgive you, then who are you to tell Him that His forgiveness is not enough? Yes, yes, Jesus died a horrible death on the cross in order to take away the sin of the world…but *your* sin was so bad that His death didn't actually pay the whole bill? God sacrificing His Son for your sins was not *quite* enough? Really? Does that make sense to you? Well! Now that I put it *that* way; it doesn't make sense to me either.

Then why, in Heaven's name, do we refuse to forgive ourselves? I've come up with a couple of answers; you pick the one you like the best. As I explained in my chapter on Agonizing Guilt, we are taught from an early age that people who do bad things must: say they are sorry, (whether they feel like it or not), they must be punished, and they must *show* how sorry they are with a sad face, drooped shoulders, and tears, if possible. Sound familiar? "Let the punishment fit the crime!" Generations of families are raised on big doses of guilt and remorse. If you haven't wallowed in depression, guilt, and self-hatred for the designated amount of time, then you must not have been very sorry in the first place! Wow! I can see my grandmother giving me the evil eye as we speak!

The other answer is harder to recognize. It's the Martyr's Syndrome. Don't try to look it up, it's my own invention. These martyrs get a sense of satisfaction by wallowing in self-pity. Now, none of them would ever admit to enjoying the guilt. That would be crazy! But they often see themselves as the victim of their own sin. "I know I messed up and ruined my marriage, but I couldn't help it! My husband was never home and I was stuck alone all day with three little children. When I met Steve at the park we just instantly connected. We could tell each other anything…"

If you find yourself saying that you *can't* forgive yourself, I want you to change one word in your self-talk. Change *can't* to *won't*. Because that makes a whole lot more sense then telling God that His forgiveness isn't enough in your case.

Forgiveness is giving up the feelings that tell you that you have the right to revenge.

Let me reassure you that vengeful feelings are normal and human. Our society calls for revenge when a wrong is committed. We are told it is right. As human beings, we feel the right to revenge deep in our souls.

We want revenge. The bad guy owes the victim a debt, and we feel that somehow, some way, he must pay it back. We rehearse and rehearse what happened in our minds. We rehearse what we *should* have said, what we *should* have done, what we *will* say to the creep if we ever have the chance. We want the bad guy to go to prison, pay money, suffer a terrible life, and/or grovel.

But God tells us to forgive our enemies. He tells us that He will take care of the revenge, and the justice. Forgiving can be a very difficult command to obey when God is asking you to forgive the man who raped you! God is not asking you to pretend that it didn't happen. By all means, call the police! Send that man to prison! My beloved, send him to prison because such people need to pay the consequences of their crime, not because you need revenge for what that man did to you.

Forgiveness is canceling the debt; writing off the loss.

You have all heard the old saying, "Forgive and forget." What a stupid thing to say! You never forget such things! You may stuff the memories away in an effort to protect yourself from the horror, but you never really forget. God is asking you to bring that debt which is owed, to Him. Please remember that no matter what happens to that person who has harmed you, it can never be paid back. Your father may suddenly become every girls' dream of what a father should be, but he can't give you back the years he was an abusive drunk. The campus jock who date-raped you may have turned his life over to Jesus and gone on to be a sincere man of God, but he cannot give you back the years of shame, humiliation, and fear you felt. You are owed a debt that no human being can repay. You need to place the debt at the foot of the cross, let go of the pain, and allow God to handle the payment plan. That way, the person owes God; not you. You can walk away assured that the perfect payment will be made; in full.

Forgiveness is not excusing.

Forgiveness is not making an excuse for someone's behavior! Forgiveness is not minimizing what happened. "Oh, he didn't mean to beat me up. He was drunk and I made him mad. He's sorry now." He'll be sorry the next time, too…and the next. Don't say that it's all right that someone injured you either mentally or physically. It is *not* all right! Women often fall into the trap of wanting to "fix" the hurt of their man by allowing selfish, sometimes brutal behavior. The thought is that "If I always show him love, by going along with whatever he wants to do. If I prove to him that not all women are out to use him, by never expecting anything for myself, then he will learn to trust and to love me as much as I love him. If I put up with his screaming rages and ridiculous demands, then he will eventually see that he is hurting me, and stop." Good luck with that! How's that been working out for you so far?

How many excuses for adultery have you heard over the years? "My wife and I: haven't gotten along for years, haven't had sex in months, fight all the time, live like room mates or (here's the best one) have an *understanding.*" There is no excuse for adultery! If your marriage is that bad then go to a marriage counselor and figure it out. If your spouse has committed adultery you need to forgive, but do not make an excuse for the sin. Excuses are only thinly veiled lies and your brain knows a lie when it hears it! So does God…by the way.

God is asking us to hand those injuries to Him, and to let Him take care of the justice that must be done. "Revenge is *mine* says the Lord."

Forgiveness is piling those hurts at the foot of the cross and walking away.

Why must we forgive this creep who has hurt us so badly? Because God has forgiven us first. Because we can totally trust God to administer justice perfectly. Because resentments are destructive and cause deep roots of bitterness. Because forgiveness is the path to God's best. Forgiveness has nothing to do with making the creep feel better; forgiveness is entirely for our own benefit.

When we are emotionally injured, we carry that wound in the form of bitterness and resentment. Resentment sits like a boulder in the pit of our stomachs, growing heavier and heavier as time goes by. Other boulders are added to the pit as other hurts go un-forgiven. The burden gets larger; the resentment goes deeper, until it affects every aspect of our lives. We find it hard to trust, to love fully, to feel at peace, to be satisfied with life. We have an inner voice constantly screaming, "This isn't right! This isn't fair!" We look for ways to ease the pain, often turning to drugs, alcohol, or sex as the remedy. Nothing really helps for very long. We must forgive the criminal so that we can let go of the bitterness, boulder by boulder, and live with the sense of joy that God intended for us.

We forgive so that we can mourn the loss we have suffered at the hands of someone else, and then move on, leaving the past where it belongs. True forgiveness can only happen with God's help, so start your journey at the foot of the cross, where all forgiveness began.

The only remedy for a wrong committed against you, is forgiveness.

The cure then, my beloved reader, starts and ends with God. He has provided all that we need to clear ourselves of both legitimate guilt and self-inflicted guilt. He alone

"…is able to do far more abundantly beyond all that we ask or think,…"
(NASB)

For those of you who are ready to go deeper.

The Method

"…that if you confess with your mouth Jesus as Lord, and believe in your heart that God raised Him from the dead, you shall be saved;" (NASB)

I want to pass on the method I use with my clients that helps them to unload the baggage they have carried for so long. This method deals with all kinds of resentments, or baggage, not just with guilt related issues. I was taught the basics of this technique by Pastor Tim Perrin, and I use it here with his permission.

A resentment is formed when a person of significance injures you emotionally. Perhaps your father constantly ignored you when you were a child. Maybe your mother called you stupid all the time and said that you were never going to amount to anything. As a child, it is nearly impossible to process emotional hurts properly. A child rarely is able to look at Daddy and think, "Well, he really loves me. He just ignores me because his father was unemotional and never showed him any affection." Unfortunately, a child's response is usually something closer to, "Daddy doesn't love me. I must be doing something wrong. I must be unlovable."

As I mentioned in the last chapter, think of that resentment as a boulder in the pit of your stomach. The boulder sits there, waiting to cause more pain whenever it is poked at by another emotional jab. The jabs come not only from Daddy, but also from other members of the family. Daddy is emotionally unavailable, so Mom is drinking too much to try and deal with her feelings of rejection. After Mom's had a few, she becomes verbally abusive to you because you are the youngest and therefore you make the most mistakes. Mom calls you vile names and wonders why she ever had you in the first place. Again, a child is going to internalize these hurtful remarks. "Mommy says that I'm a big fat baby, and that I don't have the sense God gave an onion. If I try harder to be a good girl, maybe she'll love me and stop yelling all the time." Add another boulder to the pile. In dysfunctional families, that pile of rocks can get pretty heavy, very quickly.

There are seven core values that you need to adopt in order for this method to really become part of your life: surrender, confession, transformation, reconciliation, renewal, life skills, and stewardship.

Surrender begins the process of trading in pride and self-will for humility and submission. If you have not already done so, now is the time to turn over your whole life to God through His Son, Jesus Christ. What you are doing is making admissions to God: admissions of your spiritual poverty, admissions of your powerlessness over destructive cycles, and admissions of your responsibility for your sin.

Surrender is recognition of your need for a Savior and handing your life over to God and His ways. If you can't point to a time in your life when you have made that commitment, then pray this prayer right now. It's as easy as ABC: admit, believe, commit.

Lord Jesus, I admit that I am a sinner and I am sorry for the things I have done wrong in my life. (Take a moment to confess any particular sins that are on your conscience right now) *Please forgive me. I turn my back on everything I know to be sin.*

Thank you Jesus that you died on the cross as payment for my sins. Thank you that I am forgiven and set free. I believe with my whole heart that your sacrifice was full payment for my sins.

I ask now that you come into my life by the Holy Spirit. I can't understand exactly what you have planned for me, but I commit my life to serving God and to doing His will to the best of my ability. In Your Holy and precious name, amen.

It is just that simple. Welcome to the family! There are no exact words that must be said, God is looking for what's in your heart. He knows what you mean.

Confession is trading dishonesty and secrecy for truthfulness and openness. Most of us have spent the majority of our lives keeping secrets. Family secrets can go on for generations. Secrets are driven by fear. The fear of "what will people think" is a powerful force in many people's lives. We are afraid of being judged as a bad mother, bad wife, bad Christian, and as an overall bad person. "If people knew what was really going on, they wouldn't like me." The big cover-up goes on for years and years until, often, we can't tell truth from lies anymore. The truth is that we can't walk the straight and narrow if we are always looking to other people for love and acceptance.

<u>The truth is that you are already totally loved and accepted by God. He loves you simply because you exist, not because of anything you have or have not done.</u>

Now it is time to work on some of those boulders you have been carrying around. Choose a trusted person to go through this with you. That person may be a pastor, a counselor, or a best friend. Our church has designated people who have been through the steps themselves and who have committed to helping others. This is not something you should do on your own, so find that trusted helper.

Make a list of every significant person in your life. This list may include: family members, teachers, pastors, best friends, the bully at school Anyone who influenced your life, good or bad, in a significant way. Now, go to step two:

Put a check mark beside everyone who hurt you in some way. Just a check mark, the details will be handled in step three:

Write the story of how that person injured you. Start with whomever you want, but don't leave out any details. This is the most important part, and the hardest. Go back to the earliest memory you have with that person and then, with glaring honesty, chronicle as much of the event as you can remember. Be brutally honest about what was said or done and especially be truthful about what you felt at the time. If it takes ten pages to tell all that your drunken mother said and did to you, then so be it. Get it all in writing so that you can bring those incidents and the emotions they caused in you out into the light. You have done a good job of holding onto those hurts, but they have lived in darkness long enough. Fear is fed in darkness. Mushrooms of fear grow strong and powerful in the moist dark pit where your secrets live. Once you expose them to the light, they will shrivel and die. Now comes the crucial part, step four:

Tell a trusted friend or counselor. It is extremely important that you be able to tell your story, without judgment, to another human being. Likewise, it is vitally important that you can be confident that the person you have chosen will keep your story strictly confidential. You are not looking for a friend who will feel sorry for you. "You poor thing! I can't believe your mother was so awful to you! No wonder your life has been such a mess! If I were you, I'd stop talking to that woman entirely. That'll show her!" Those kinds of words may seem supportive, but in the long run they are just feeding your anger. Your resentments need to be shared with a person who is mostly going to listen. There is something about saying the words out loud that helps to dislodge that boulder. When those events are spoken of and looked at in the clear light of day, they lose some of their power. Fear is weakened. Once you have spoken of all the hurts that were inflicted onto you by, let's say Mom, then you and your partner are ready to move to step five:

Pray to God, telling Him that you want to forgive that person. I want to emphasize some points about forgiveness so that you might have a clearer understanding of what God is asking you to do when He tells you to forgive.

Mom owes you a debt. That debt is a loving, safe, happy childhood. No child deserves to be treated the way you were treated. Don't try to minimize the debt by making excuses for Mom. There is no excuse. We are all responsible for our behavior regardless of our past. Telling yourself that you are going to forgive Mom because she had a lousy marriage and she didn't really mean to say those horrible things isn't going to get rid of the anger. Your brain knows a lie when it hears it and you just told a whopper. **Making excuses for someone is not forgiveness**. That debt is sitting in your gut in the shape of a boulder. That boulder is made out of fear, anger, pain, and resentment. *The debt can never be repaid by Mom!*

Even if Mom suddenly changes her behavior and showers you with love and acceptance, *she can never give you back the childhood you deserved.* Beloved, God is asking you to release that debt to Him. He is asking you to let go of the dream you cling to, the dream in which, somehow, Mom makes it all up to you. That time in your life cannot be "made up" for, the childhood years are over. No human being can pay the debt; no human being can fill that hole in your heart.

I tell my clients to visualize that boulder of resentment. I ask them to see themselves taking that boulder and placing it at the foot of the cross. Take that hurt and leave it with God, where it belongs. Let go of that anger and the desire you have for revenge and let God replace it with His peace. You've held onto it long enough.

Tell God that you want to forgive Mom, naming each specific hurt, and then thank Him for taking the pain from you. Now, turn your back on that boulder and leave it where you placed it, at the foot of the cross.

Repeat the prayer of forgiveness with each person on your list. Remember, be specific. This process usually takes many sessions with my clients. Don't worry about how long it takes. You probably will remember other people and other hurts as you go through your list; just add them to your paper and pray through it.

Bringing up past hurts can be very disturbing at times. Sometimes you will feel worse than when you started. Don't panic. That is a normal reaction. If you had a cancer growing on your nose the doctor would want to cut it out. After surgery that spot would be very painful and you might think that this pain wasn't worth it, after all, the cancer didn't hurt before the surgery. But we all understand that if we ignore cancer, sooner or later, it will kill us. Remember the last time you had the flu? You felt nauseated, it got worse and worse until you finally ran to the bathroom and vomited. The act of throwing up was no fun either. It tasted terrible coming out, but after you were done throwing up you probably said to yourself, "Whew! I feel better now, what a relief." Getting rid of these resentments can be very much like throwing up. In the beginning you actually feel worse, later you are relieved.

Sometimes we experience pain during a healing process. Don't be afraid of the pain these memories may cause, the pain will diminish with time. You need to grieve the loss you suffered. Grief eventually leads to healing. Boulders of resentment never heal, they never diminish, they just get added onto until they choke the very life out of us.

Once you have gone through the whole "hurts" inventory it is time to move on to the next step:

Get out that same list of significant people in your life and make another check mark. This is a mark beside the name of every person on that list that *you* have injured. Whoa! Now we really are getting to the painful part! Think back to the story in this book about my ex-brother-in-law. As a result of Dave's behavior toward my sister and their children I had formed resentments against him. I had never directly fought with Dave, called him names to his face, or refused to associate with Dave. But I certainly did have a judgmental and critical attitude toward him. That leads us to the next step.

Write, in detail, your sins against the person with this second check mark. Did you gossip, slash their tires, lie about them to others, say hateful things to them, or even wish ill on them? Write it all down. Go through the whole list. Now examine what you have done. Do you see a pattern of behavior?

When I made my list of sins, I felt as if God had smacked me right in the face with the list. I clearly saw the pattern of behavior that I had followed my entire life each time I was hurt. I developed a judgmental and critical attitude toward every person on my list. What a shock! I had always thought of myself as the least judgmental person on earth. I had listened to hundreds of people over the years tell me of the horrible things they had done to others, without a thought of criticism toward them. Yet, when I was personally affected, judgment and criticism was my first reaction. I understood for the first time in my life what it meant to have a "besetting sin".

Most people have a "besetting sin" which falls into one of three categories: 1) pleasure; 2) materialism; 3) power/control. The way you can discern this is to ask the question, "Where do I turn when I feel bad?" Do you seek pleasure through sex, eating, drinking, or partying? When you are unhappy do you go on a shopping spree, buy gifts for friends, brag about your fancy car, or deposit yet another big wad of money into your savings account? Perhaps, like me, you seek to control your circumstances and the people around you.

I was angry because I couldn't control my ex-brother-in-law. I couldn't *make* him behave. If Dave, and everyone else in my life, would just do things **my** way, then everything would turn out great! It was hard to admit that my control issues were in charge of my emotional health.

Now ask God to forgive you for your sins against those people on your list. Again, be specific and pray it out loud with your trusted person present. This is no time to minimize and make excuses for yourself. Let's call a sin a sin and get rid of it.

You've done a lot of work so far! You made a list of all significant relationships, you've written out all the wrongs you have suffered at the hands of other people, you have forgiven each wrong, you have listed all the wrongs you have committed against others and asked God's forgiveness, and you have recognized the destructive patterns you fall into when you feel hurt. Good job! Now take a breath and move on to the next task when you feel ready.

Make a list of your fears. Fear is the driving force behind many of our actions. Recognizing what our fears are is the first step to getting rid of them. Here are a few fears that are very common to help you get started: fear of losing what you have, fear of rejection, fear of not getting what you want or need, fear of economic insecurity, fear of failure, fear of death, fear of God's punishment, fear of returning to destructive cycles of behavior, fear of being found out for what you really are, and fear of the consequences of previous actions. After your list is completed you can now pray this prayer;

"God, these are my fears. (name them) I am powerless over these fears. I cannot get rid of them myself. I need your help. God, please remove these fears from me and show me what You would have me be."

Good job! You are almost done, so hang in there. Now take the next courageous step:

Make a list of every person you have had sexual contact with. Ouch! For some of us that may be a long, painful, list. I know your first question, "But what if we didn't 'go all the way'?" What did you do? Did you "just kiss" a guy? If it made you feel uncomfortable, then maybe he should be on that list. Sexual contact can include heavy petting, oral sex, mutual masturbation, or intercourse. This list will include your spouse if you had relations before you were married. Now comes the next step:

Pray through your list. Yes, in front of your trusted prayer partner. The goal here is not to humiliate you, the goal is to get all of your junk out into the open, exposed to the light. Ask God to forgive you for your part in this and tell God that you want to forgive the person on the list for his part. Ask God to restore your sexual purity.

Honest confession is a spiritual tool that you must choose to use for the rest of your life. Confession is a vital and indispensable part of growth. Confession requires the verbal admission of those things about you which you have struggled to keep secret. Admissions must be made not only to God, but also to another human. The very act of revealing yourself to another person will teach you humility and honesty to a degree that you have never known before. The cleansing effect of confession will be the freeing of your soul from the tethers of secret guilt. The darkness will lift as the light of God's forgiveness shines through.

I fully understand that the very thought of confession in front of another person is terrifying. I understand such terror because I have gone through these steps myself. It was the hardest thing I have ever done. Confessing to God was not a big problem for me because I believe that He already knew what I had done and I was already forgiven. It took me years to grasp that when I confessed to God in private, I was still holding onto that sin so that I could hang onto my public image. Pride, pure and simple folks! Privacy made my sins easier to rationalize and to minimize.

It wasn't until I marched my sins out into the full light for another person to see that I was able to become accountable. When I told my confessor what had gone on in the past it gave her permission to ask me how I was doing with that problem.

Again, the warning that I must make here is that the person who hears this confession must be absolutely trustworthy and closed mouth. Great damage can be suffered if the confessor cannot keep confidences. Hearing the sins of others is a sacred trust.

I will make a promise here that you can hold me to. If you will go through this process, your fears will begin to be alleviated and you will feel a new freedom from things that have been plaguing you for years. You will definitely feel closer to God and cleaner than you have felt in a long time.

Whew! The hardest part is finished. You have entered a lifestyle of truthfulness and openness. Let's move on to core value three, transformation.

Transformation is trading the fear of change, for faith in God's purposes. Romans 12:2 says "Do not conform any longer to the pattern of this world, but be transformed by the renewing of your mind. Then you will be able to test and approve what God's will is-His good, pleasing, and perfect will." (NIV)

You have gotten a glimpse into what your particular cycles of sin are. You have listed some of your fears. Transformation cannot fully take place if you are driven by fear. Recognize the destructiveness of fear. Fear of failure causes me not to try. Fear of rejection causes me to say or do things that I know to be wrong. Recognize fear's connection to self-will. Fear is a result of a focus on created things rather than focus the Creator.

Defensiveness is a fear-driven response to the threatening presence, personality, or actions of another person. Defensiveness can be expressed in many different ways; some are very subtle. Sarcasm or teasing is the use of humor when you feel threatened. Wit can be the use of intelligence to defend oneself. Arrogance is the attempt to defend by giving off a superior demeanor. Lying is used in order to compensate for irresponsibility.

People who engage in the one-upmanship defense have a fear of being viewed as less experienced or less skilled. Seeking pity is a way of defending oneself. False humility is a means of keeping threatening people away. Flattery and acts of kindness can be a way of trying to win a person over, get on their good side. A quick temper, aggressive personality, or physical aggression is a defense to keep a perceived threat at arm's length.

Manipulation, obsessive cleanliness, gossip, and jealousy are all tactics used to control a fearful situation. Stress, anxiety, and depression come about as a response to fear and are a defense mechanism.

A person will quite often develop a repertoire of defensive strategies and rotate them. Defensiveness will hinder your integrity and is a sign of carnality.

As long as you insist on holding onto your fears, your fears will control you.

What is a person to do then? Write and pray, write and pray, write and pray. Repeat as necessary. It may sound simplistic, but it works. Let God be your defender. Real transformation will occur as God replaces fear with faith. Writing down your worst fears brings them into the light. The darkness will lift as you faithfully hand each one to the Lord. He will not harm you. God loves you with all of His heart, you can trust Him.

Transformation is a daily goal. A truly transformed life is one in which God is the first place we go for defense, help, comfort, and peace. It takes practice and patience to learn to let go of the old ways of doing things and to hand problems over to God from the start.

Our old nature keeps trying to take control, there is a constant tug-of-war. The good news is that God is able to win every time, if you will allow Him in.

In his book *The Pursuit of God*, A.W. Tozer wrote, "The labor of self-love is a heavy one indeed. Think for yourself whether much of your sorrow has not arisen from someone speaking slightly of you. As long as you set yourself up as a little god to which you must be loyal there will be those who will delight to offer affront to your idol. How then can you hope to have inward peace? The heart's fierce effort to protect itself from every slight, to shield its touchy honor from the bad opinion of friend and enemy, will never let the mind have rest."

Beloved, take the rest that God is offering to you, go to Him first.

Romans 12:18 says, "If it is possible, as far as it depends on you, live at peace with everyone." That leads us to the fourth core value, reconciliation.

Reconciliation can be a difficult step. When people are reconciled their differences are settled. Harmony is restored. Sounds good on paper, but real life pain can run pretty deep. Let me give a personal example that I am sure many of you can relate to.

My first marriage ended in divorce after eight years and one child. There is no need to go into all the gory details, but I will say that my emotional scars were deep and painful. After I accepted Jesus as my Savior, it still took several years before I was willing to forgive my ex-husband. It took several more before I understood the need for reconciliation. Forgiveness and reconciliation are brothers, but they are not identical twins.

Forgiving my ex-husband was releasing the debt that he could never pay back to me, and letting God handle that debt. Forgiveness was letting go of my vengeful thoughts and hatred for Tom. But reconciliation would mean that I was to live at peace with Tom, not just refrain from strangling him. I thought I had done enough. Why should I have to take that extra step and actually be at harmony with Tom? He didn't deserve peace with me. What was I supposed to do, call him up once a week and chat?

Reconciliation is trading ill-will and resentment for a willingness to be at peace with everyone. God was asking me to be at peace with Tom. I didn't see the need until I found out that he and his wife were coming to visit my daughter and granddaughter. Old resentments returned and I found myself fantasizing about the nasty things I would say to them if we happened to see each other. I was shocked enough at my hateful thoughts to ask my Sunday school class to pray for me. I was horrified to hear myself say to the group, "Please pray for my attitude. To tell you the truth, I wouldn't walk across the street to spit on them if they were on fire!" Several people gasped. I had not intended for those words to come out, I didn't even know they were in there! Needless to say, I spent a lot of time in prayer myself. I had to ask God to give me the desire to be at peace with Tom and his wife. I did not have the ability to feel peaceful toward them on my own.

I feel desire was the key. I had not desired to obey God's command to be at peace with everyone because I did not see, again, that it was really for my benefit. There was a black spot on my heart that I was unwilling to let go of, a secret closet that I refused to clean out. Once I had spoken those nasty words to the class, that secret was exposed to the light and I was able to see how ugly my attitude really was.

By the time Tom and his wife came to visit, I truly felt at peace with them. They did come to my house and I invited them in whole heartedly. What a relief! Did I later feel the need to call them to chat? No. They are not friends of mine. Did I tell them that I wanted to be at peace with them and that the Lord had given me that peace? No. Tom and his wife are not Christians and have made it clear, through my daughter, that they have no desire to hear anything on the subject from me.

In a previous chapter I spoke of making restitution, where appropriate. Reconciliation speaks more to making amends in current and past relationships, although that may include restitution. Sometimes the mending of past relationships can only be done in your heart. Telling Tom what I had gone through to be at peace with him would have opened up a can of worms. Other times you may have to make amends in person. Again, mature Christian counsel is invaluable here.

The whole point is that the Lord is asking you to be at peace with everyone in your own heart. If that means that a relationship can be restored then great, but if it simply means that as far as you are concerned peace has been accomplished, then that's good too. One word of caution here; be very careful that you don't avoid confronting and reconciling a relationship on the grounds that face to face contact would only cause more harm. If God is telling you to go to someone personally, then don't make excuses. That is another reason why having the counsel of a trusted, mature, Christian is so very important. We humans love to rationalize. All of these steps have paved the way to our next core value; renewal.

Now that most of the garbage in your heart has been dealt with, it is time to replace the old way of doing things with new patterns. The Bible makes it quite clear that after we have swept out the dirt, we need to put something into that clean room or the dirt will simply return. Much of your bad behavior and incorrect ways of dealing with life have become habits. Habits are learned behavior, and therefore can be unlearned. However, unless you replace the bad habit with a good habit your mind and emotions will naturally regress back to the familiar.

Renewal is trading avoidance and spiritual laziness for openness and discipline. How many Christians do you know who are spiritually complacent? Oh sure, they go to church every Sunday, participate in fund raising projects and tithe every month, but the joy and excitement of living a life filled with the Holy Spirit has somehow faded away. The spark that once lit up their eyes is now a dim flicker. Complacent Christians are a very sad sight and all too common. Why not live the abundant life that Jesus came to earth to give to us?

Jesus gave us a perfect roadmap for having that renewal everyday. Look at Matthew chapter six starting in verse five. First, Jesus tells us that just repeating a bunch of words over and over is silly and useless, then He tells us how to pray. Jesus clearly does not mean that we are to repeat His exact words. Jesus is showing us the elements of meaningful prayer, that deep heart-felt prayer while we are alone with God.

Begin your prayer with worship. Use the psalms, or sometimes hymns, to remind you of God's greatness and goodness. You will become like whom you love and adore the most. Worship prepares the will for surrender to God's purposes.

Pray for God's purposes to be accomplished. Remind yourself of the reason you are here on earth; for His purposes to be accomplished through you and to worship God. Think about what God is doing around you. Now think about how you can join God in His Kingdom work.

Pray for your needs to be met. Even if you are prosperous, acknowledge that all things come from God. Ask God for everything, even if you already have the resources. Pray for God to help you with financial decisions. Most importantly, ask God to show you the difference between wants and needs.

Pray for forgiveness. You need to do a daily inventory of your sins as well as those sins committed against you. This prevents the resentments from piling up and keeps that communication path with the Lord clear of obstacles. Recognize the connection between God's forgiveness and your willingness to forgive every day.

Pray against temptation. Recognize God's power over the evil one. Notice that we are asking that God would keep us from walking toward temptation rather than giving us strength in the face of it. We not only show our love and commitment to God in the choices we make during a crisis, but also in what we do to avoid getting into that situation in the first place. You've done your inventory, you know where your weak areas are, ask God to bring to your mind the actions you need to take *today* to avoid your temptation areas.

Give God the glory! Re-affirm your desire to place your life in His care as you start this day.

If you will get into the habit of praying to your heavenly Father everyday, your spiritual blessings will be too numerous to count.

Now that you have spoken to God, give Him a chance to speak back. Bible study is a precious communion with God for some and a grinding bore for others. Most of us have been on both sides of that fence. The fact remains that the Lord most often speaks to us through His word. The Lord has communicated audibly with me three times in my life. I can never express how precious those times are to me, but three times in more than fifty years is hardly an active chat-room.

God gave us His word so that we might know Him. Think of the Bible as a personal letter from your Father to you. Ask Him to speak to you personally as you open His word each day. If there is a message the Lord wants you to understand, I can promise you that a certain verse or passage will jump right out at you.

Bible study with a group is critical to your growth as a Christian. Whole worlds will open up as people of different maturity levels share their thoughts on a passage.

The Bible tells us not to forsake the gathering together with one another. That leads us to the final step in our renewal process; attending a church. If I had a nickel for every person who told me that they didn't need to go to church, I'd be a rich woman. The excuses are all the same; "I don't need some religious organization telling me how to worship God.", "Church is full of hypocrites.", "I worship God in my own way." "Church is boring, the music puts me to sleep." "Sunday is a day of rest. I'm sleeping in."

Name the excuse, I've heard it. The truth is that God wants us to worship together, to encourage each other, to exhort each other, to help each other, to learn together, and to be accountable.

To be accountable; that bears repeating. When we are in the middle of sinning, or even thinking about it, we don't want any nosey Christians asking personal questions. Darkness hates the light. After more than twenty-five years of lay counseling I can tell you that when a Christian marriage is in trouble and one or both people don't want to face their own sin in the issues, the first thing that happens is they stop coming to church. The excuse is usually busyness, then they are visiting other churches because they've grown tired of this Pastor, and pretty soon they have dropped out of sight completely. It is a painful process to watch and all too common. As Christians we need to be accountable to other Christians and the best way to do that is through a local church. The varieties are endless here in the United States, so there is no excuse for not finding one that suits your needs. Just make sure that it is a church that uses the Bible as its guide.

Life skills is core value number six. You have done a great deal of changing throughout this book. Old ways of thinking, poor choices, have been dealt with and you are ready to move on. But move on to where? It takes planning and skill to replace bad habits with good choices. An entire book could be written on this subject alone, but I will just touch on a few basics.

Temptation must be dealt with on an almost daily basis. In making this tremendous effort to live a transformed life, one of the things you have surely done is to get the attention of Satan. He didn't need to bother you much while you were wallowing in your own sin. He hates it when people are walking with God! You don't need to fear Satan, he is nothing compared to God, but you do need to be aware of his tricks.

Let's say you are an alcoholic. You have been sober for six months now and your relationships are starting to heal. Then one evening, out of the blue, an old drinking buddy shows up at your door with a bottle of your favorite booze. Is that temptation from God? Is He testing you to see if you *really* meant it when you asked Him to help you stop drinking? I can tell you that the temptation is not from God. Scripture says; "Let no one say when he is tempted, 'I am being tempted by God', for God cannot be tempted by evil, and He Himself does not tempt anyone. But each one is tempted when he is carried away and enticed by his own lust. Then when lust has conceived, it gives birth to sin;…" (NASB) For an alcoholic, drinking is a sin.

You need a plan, Stan. Look ahead at the "what ifs". What if I'm invited to the office Christmas party? Should I go? What is my plan for staying sober at a party? What if I run into an old friend and he invites me out for a drink? Should I go or should I suggest we meet at a coffee shop? You will be presented with countless temptations. You must plan how to handle those temptations **before** they present themselves.

Part of new life skills will be learning how to have healthy relationships. If you grew up in a dysfunctional home and have had unhealthy relationships as an adult, then you must learn what a healthy relationship looks like, how to develop a good relationship, and how to maintain it. These are not easy skills to learn. The best advice I can give is to take advantage of the resources around you. *Boundaries* by Dr. Henry Cloud and Dr. John Townsend is an excellent book on the subject and many churches have classes based on this book.

Many churches have parenting classes, marriage building seminars, and Christian family living Bible studies. Make it a priority to go to some of theses classes. Learn from watching how a family you admire functions. Don't be afraid to ask questions of mature Christians. What you will find is that we all have struggles, there is no such thing as a perfect family. God has shown us the way to healthy relationships if we will just open our hearts to Him.

Last but not least of our core values is stewardship. "I knew it! Church people eventually get around to asking for money!" Well, stewardship certainly does include the proper perspective on money, but that is not all it entails. God has given you life. At the moment of your salvation you were also given certain spiritual gifts.

Stewardship is learning to give away what God has given to you. Stewardship is trading gravity for grace.

We often insist on holding onto things we possess such as; money, time, skills, and spiritual gifts. We act much like a two-year-old clutching a pile of toys so the other children can't play with them. Mine, mine, mine! Funny thing is, that two-year-old is so busy trying to protect his stuff he doesn't get any fun out of the toys either. That child is stuck to that spot, unable to move because he is afraid to let go. As adults we do the same thing with our money, gifts, and time. What we don't realize is that we are really missing out on the abundant life that God has promised.

A life full of the need to possess can be traded for a life full of opportunity and satisfaction. I would much rather feel that I was accomplishing something for God than using what He has given me for my own selfish desires. God isn't going to force you to give up your toys, but if you truly love Him you will gladly share.

That's it! I've said my piece! Thank you for hanging in there with me. I want to invite you to write me. I have an online advice column. Visit my website, www.guiltlady.com. Read some questions and answers and then email me with your own questions or comments.

A life free from guilt is not only attainable, but also something God desires for you. An abundant life starts and ends with Jesus Christ. He has provided the way through His love and His sacrifice. That new life is being held out to you, right now, as a gift from God. All you have to do is grab hold of it.

"Be anxious for nothing, but in everything by prayer and supplication with thanksgiving let your requests be made known to God. And the peace of God, which surpasses all comprehension, shall guard your hearts and your minds in Christ Jesus." (NASB)